COMMUNION
with the
FRIENDS OF
GOD

COMMUNION
with the
FRIENDS OF
GOD

Meditations and Prayers from
Women Mystics

JANE MCAVOY

Chalice Press®
St. Louis, Missouri

All scripture quotations, unless otherwise indicated, are from the *New Revised Standard Version Bible,* copyright 1989, division of Christian Education of the National Council of the Churches of Christ in the United States of America. Used by permission.

Cover art: Detail from "Summer: Harvesters in the Field" by Pieter Brueghel, the Elder © Christie's Images/SuperStock
Cover design: Wendy Barnes
Interior design: Elizabeth Wright
Art direction: Elizabeth Wright

This book is printed on acid-free, recycled paper.

Visit Chalice Press on the World Wide Web at
www.chalicepress.com

10 9 8 7 6 5 4 3 2 1   01 02 03 04 05

Library of Congress Cataloging-in-Publication Date

McAvoy, Jane Ellen, 1957–
    Communion with the friends of God : meditations and prayers from women mystics / Jane McAvoy.
        p. cm.
    Includes bibliographical references and indexes.
    ISBN 0-8272-0484-1 (pbk. : alk. paper)
    1. Women mystics—Biography. 2. Spiritual life—Christianity.   I. Title
BV5095.A1 M39 2001
242—dc21   2001000776

Printed in the United States of America

CONTENTS

Preface   vii

Introduction   1

1. Laying Down Our Burdens   11

2. Confessing Our Sins   31

3. Celebrating Our Savior   51

4. Standing with Our Sister Mary   71

5. Growing Our Souls   87

6. Sharing Our Sorrows   105

Bibliography   127

Index of Hymns and Readings   129

Index of Scripture References   133

PREFACE

I am grateful to Chalice Press for their excitement about this project and in particular to Jon L. Berquist for his editorial advice. My thanks also goes to Lexington Theological Seminary for a sabbatical leave to work on this project. This book is dedicated to all those elders who have enriched my celebration of communion by their heartfelt prayers and meditations. For Janie, Charlie, Kenney, Anne, Greg, Barb, Buster, Mark, Ruth Ann, and countless others who have led the people of God in the celebration of communion, I give thanks.

INTRODUCTION

Communing with the Friends of God

Week after week, many people who sit in church and listen to the prayers before communion hear mumbled prayers of thanks for the salvation offered through the sacrifice of Jesus. At times I sense that our hearts may not be in these prayers. My hunch is that they are trying to make sense of the celebration of a body broken for our sins, but they do not quite know what to celebrate. The death of an innocent victim hardly seems like something to celebrate, and if that death is somehow our fault, it hardly seems a memory that can save us. As a result, our prayers are laced with halfhearted platitudes that elicit respect, guilt, and confession, but fail to articulate the mystery of salvation.

The problem is the belief that we have to glorify sacrifice at the communion table. In the book *Saving Jesus,* Carter Heyward argues that God is not satisfied by obedience, but by efforts to honor our own and other's bodies. Likewise, I want to claim that saving communion will not come about by being obedient to an outdated understanding of sacrificial atonement, but will be reborn by honoring the living Body of Christ that encourages our bodies and the Body of Christ to live. There is a way to celebrate the salvation offered in Jesus Christ, and it is not by glorifying sacrifice, but by understanding the satisfying love that is offered to us by God in Christ.

At communion, we give voice to our understanding of salvation, what theologians call atonement. The most common doctrine of atonement is based on the idea that Christ's death pays the debt for our sins; in short, Christ's death satisfies God. But what if God does not need satisfaction? What if the problem is our need to be satisfied, not God's need to be placated? Then the answer to this need is not the crucifixion of a sacrificial lamb, but the incarnation of God's love. This view of salvation is just what the medieval mystic Julian of Norwich believed. She wrote that satisfaction is a human need; it is

1

the need to be satisfied that God loves us. Salvation is accepting this love from God, and Christ is the vehicle of this acceptance. The satisfaction of God's love is what the prodigal son received; satisfying love is what we need; and communion is the place to receive and celebrate satisfaction. At communion, we confess our need for satisfaction, we celebrate God's saving grace, and we participate in God's saving love.

This book follows the train of thought that I began in my book *The Satisfied Life*, in which I describe how the writings of medieval women mystics can help us understand satisfaction as God's saving love.[1] In this book of meditations and prayers, I want to suggest that we can learn from their lives and writings how to celebrate communion as an experience of God's saving grace. It may seem odd for a Protestant to base a book of communion meditations and prayers on the writings of Christian saints. Here, I am following the lead of Elizabeth Johnson, who calls the communion of saints the friends and prophets of God.[2] Communion with the saints is about the way in which we connect with holy people in holy moments, especially at the celebration of the service of communion. They are part of the great cloud of witnesses that the book of Hebrews commends to us as inspiration for the life of faith (Hebrews 12:1–2).

I have been drawn to the writings of medieval women mystics because of their witness to the living reality of communion. Women mystics in particular are drawn to communion, in part because of their exclusion from priestly office. At communion they could experience an immediate connection with God and a way of affirming their status in the church. Thus, they are witnesses to the way in which communion can strengthen and empower us, as well as reminders of the full ambiguity of salvation in the face of injustice. In remembering their lives, Johnson suggests that we bring the subversive, encouraging, liberating power of their witness to our lives.

My denomination, the Christian Church (Disciples of Christ), shares this focus on communion and the experience of the laity. For

---

[1]Jane McAvoy, *The Satisfied Life: Medieval Women Mystics on Atonement* (Cleveland: The Pilgrim Press, 2000).

[2]Elizabeth Johnson, *Friends of God and Prophets: A Feminist Theological Reading of the Communion of Saints* (New York: Continuum, 1998).

Disciples, communion is the center of the worship service. That is why every worship service includes the celebration of communion. It is understood as a time of personal reflection and prayer in which one seeks to be at one with God. While it is common for the ordained minister to offer a communion meditation, lay elders preside at the table and offer the communion prayer. Usually two elders preside at the table, one offering a prayer for the bread and the other a prayer for the cup, or one offering the communion prayer and the other reciting the words of institution. Although the order of the service can vary, the importance of the elders symbolizes the Disciples' emphasis on the role of the laity.

But it would be an overstatement to say that these medieval women mystics would feel at home in a modern-day Disciples service. It is hard to translate the insights of medieval women mystics to our day without making the women appear to be just like us or trapping them in a distant and foreign world. While I understand the communion service to elicit the memory of God's saving love in Christ, they understood themselves literally to be eating the body and blood of Christ. The depth of their communion experience made sense in the midst of their religious tradition, while it seems strange and exotic to me.

We must be careful to remember that they are witnesses to a practice of communion that is shaped by medieval times and distant places. We can learn best from them by naming the real joys and struggles of their lives, by bearing witness to how communion inspired, compelled, comforted and troubled them, and by discovering the corresponding themes that we face in our lives. Their witness points us to the fullness of communion that we long for and rarely realize. Like them we are devout participants in an ancient ritual that has transforming potential. From them we may be able to catch a vision of a practice of communion that we truly can celebrate.

Six Medieval Women Mystics

This book of meditations and prayers is built on the lives and writings of six women who lived during the Middle Ages, from the eleventh to the fourteenth centuries. They lived in different places and different times but shared a passion for the Christian life and a desire to be at one with God. A few were well-known church leaders in their day; others are known to us only because their writings were passed down through the ages. One was married and had fourteen children; the rest joined some form of the religious life. They share the title mystic because their writings bear witness to a tangible sense of the presence of God.

Julian of Norwich, who first inspired me with the idea that satisfaction is the gift of God's love, lived in England in the plague-torn era of the fourteenth century. She had seen much sickness and almost died from some form of the plague. In the midst of her illness she had a series of revelations—we might call them visions or dreams—that gave her a new understanding of the meaning of salvation. This insight was based on a story of a Lord who shows unconditional love for his servant. When the servant falls during an effort to do the Lord's work, the Lord does not punish the servant, but takes pity on him and sends another servant to rescue him from distress. This is the story of our lives. We are the servants who are rescued by our master through the benevolent work of the servant who is God's son. Julian describes this devotion as being like a mother's love and is probably best known for her very modern-sounding idea that Jesus is our Mother. Through her we can begin to think about how communion is the celebration of the gracious love of God.

This theme of love is further developed by the writings of Mechthild of Magdeburg. Mechthild lived in the thirteenth century during a time of great opportunity for religious women. She was part of a group called the beguines, who devoted their lives to service and love of God. Unlike nuns, who were often cloistered behind convent walls, beguines lived in the world and showed their love for God by caring for the sick, the orphaned, and the distressed. Like all free spirits, beguines received a great deal of criticism from church leaders and local people. Mechthild's writings are filled with the passion of her love, the struggle to endure persecution, and the constant quest for communion with God.

Another beguine is Hadewijch of Brabant, who was the leader of a beguine community. Much of her writing is filled with advice for living a life of service and devotion. Her letters reveal a practical understanding of the delicate balance required of those who strive to be in the world, but not bound by its expectations or values. Hadewijch uses poetry as a vehicle to describe this alternate life as a love affair with God. Her poems are filled with images of Christ as a Lady of Love and her soul as a knight dedicated to Love's service. Underneath this romantic imagery is a profound sense of how love for God can lead to a life of devout service. Her own life of service was fueled by a profound spiritual life that centered on the celebration of communion. It was at these times that she experienced the fulfillment of her love.

Another woman of great service was Hildegard of Bingen, who was a nun, abbess, poet, theologian, musician, and prophet. She established two new convents in Germany during the twelfth century and was an active participant in church reform. She is known today for her theological books, which emphasize the goodness of creation and our place within it. She had a unique way of writing that included drawing pictures of her theological ideas. One such image depicts salvation as the light of Christ slowly overcoming the darkness of evil in the world. She saw this saving work continuing in our own lives as we work for harmony and justice with all of creation. Communion was a symbol of this harmony as the wholeness of Christ entered the wholeness of creation through the worship of the whole church.

Margery Kempe is a lesser-known woman. In fact, some would argue she has no place in a list of Christian mystics. A contemporary of Julian who reportedly asked Julian for advice, Margery was troubled about the conflict between her desire for a religious life and her responsibilities as a wife and mother. Julian urged her to trust her instincts and trust God. Margery's search for love and acceptance led her on a series of pilgrimages to sacred sites around the world. Her religious devotion verged on fanaticism, and she was often criticized for her religious outbursts. But Margery's quest for communion and her relentless search for the satisfaction of God's love were genuine. She symbolizes the longing and the struggle for the assurance of acceptance as a child of God.

Best known of all these mystics is Catherine of Siena, who lived during one of the most corrupt times in the church's history and bore witness to a love for God that would not flinch in the face of suffering. She struggled with her family for control of her life, fought to end conflicts between families in her community, worked to bring unity to a divided church, and ministered to the sick during three outbreaks of the plague. In the midst of all this strife, she came to understand Christ's patient endurance of suffering as a model for our lives, and the nourishment offered by Christ in communion as the medicine that heals our sorrows. It is Catherine who shows the way to acknowledge both the suffering of the world and the satisfying love of God in Christ.

Communion as Confession, Celebration, and Commission

If we could sit around the table with these six women, they would have much to tell us about communion. I have organized the wisdom from their writings around six themes that explore aspects of the meaning of salvation that we experience in the celebration of communion. No one theme is sufficient to name the mystery of God's satisfying love, but together they describe the richness of communion with God.

The first theme is laying down our burdens at communion. We come to the communion table with the weight of the world on our shoulders; yet rarely do we acknowledge the pain and suffering of our lives. Communion is a place to give voice to these burdens and lay them to rest at the table. Like Margery, Christians come to the table with the pain of rejection, or like Hildegard we struggle with physical pain. Hadewijch gives voice to the burden of persecution and betrayal, while Catherine struggles with church politics. Julian expresses the self-doubt that bears on our souls, and Mechthild agonizes over the absence of God. Communion is the place to lay down our burdens and rest in God.

Communion is also the place to confess our sins. Until we give voice to the sins that keep us from receiving God's love, we will not be able to commune. Julian describes sin as blindness to our identity as children of God. Catherine confesses that her own self-loathing led to her abusing her body to the point of starvation. Margery confesses the shame of adultery that clouds her soul, and Mechthild talks of the pride and anger that keep her from God. Hildegard understood the way in which neglect of the earth is a sin against God. Communion is the opportunity to confess our sins and ask for forgiveness from an ever-loving God.

The joy of communion is the celebration of the redeeming work of Christ. The variety of ways in which these women describe Christ opens up our imaginations to the magnitude of salvation. Julian describes Christ as our Mother, the One who feeds our souls in communion bread and wine. He is also a Gardener who tends to our souls so that we can grow into God's love. Catherine imagines Christ as a Bridge who provides the way for us to meet God. Margery hears Christ's gentle words of comfort and assurance, Hadewijch describes the magnitude of this love, and Mechthild gives thanks for the steadfastness of Christ's presence as our Fellow Sufferer. At communion, we see, we taste, and we give voice to salvation in our lives.

One of the most interesting and unusual themes in the writing of medieval women is their relationship with Mary as the role model of salvation. The chapter "Standing with our Sister Mary" explores the way in which Mary is a window to the saving work of God. This theme may be the most foreign to Protestant readers, especially in light of Roman Catholic declarations about the conception and assumption of Mary. I am reminded of Jaroslav Pelikan's book *Mary Through the Centuries*, which traces the role of Mary through Christian history.[3] He writes that Mary is a woman for all seasons who today is seen less as mediator of salvation and more as model of faith.

Medieval women identified with Mary's courage, action, and relentless faith. Margery thinks of Mary as her sister and strives to emulate Mary's courageous faithfulness to her savior, even as he is raised on the cross. Mechthild speaks of Mary as the wife of God, an odd notion to us, but one that gives voice to the intimacy of love. Hadewijch speaks of the power of Mary's humility that could possess a part of God. She contemplates what it could mean to tap into this same power in our lives. Hildegard expands the image of Mary to one that represents Mother Church, Mother Earth, and the power of Justice. Standing in the midst of these feminine images expands our understanding of the magnitude of the saving work of God.

Communion becomes an opportunity not only to receive but also to respond to God's love. "Growing our Souls" is a collection of ways in which we can participate in the saving love of God. Hildegard is famous for the idea that our souls are like gardens that bloom in God. She describes this process as the greening of our souls. For Hildegard, this growth opens us to the ladder of virtue that flows between our hearts and God. Hadewijch praises the glory of noble service to God, service that can lead to a relationship of companionship and struggle with God. Margery is challenged to

---

[3]Jaroslav Pelikan, *Mary Through the Centuries: Her Place in the History of Culture* (New Haven, Conn.: Yale University Press, 1996).

imagine a life that balances her many roles as mother, sister, and wife as part of, rather than distractions from, her devotion to God. Julian reminds us that this growth is a healing process that turns bitterness into hope. Communion nourishes our souls and challenges us to grow in faith.

The concluding chapter suggests ways in which communion empowers us to share the sorrows of the world. Hadewijch is struck by the way in which communion forces us to think beyond ourselves to the community of faith. Julian reminds us that this community is a blessing that can lift up the sorrows of any one of its members. Hildegard understands the communion table to be something that opens us up to the quest for justice in the world, while Margery expresses the frustration in this quest in her tears for the world. Catherine sees the blood of Christ symbolized at the communion table as an image of the interconnectedness of our lives to our world and to God. It is because of this connection that we share the sorrows of the world and yet remain confident in the ultimate victory of God's saving love. With this victory, we catch a glimpse of the completion of salvation in an eschatological table that stands before us in faith.

Suggestions for Worship and Personal Reflection

Worship leaders may use this book in worship services. Each entry begins with a quote followed by an explanation of its meaning and meditation, which could be used in the worship service. The prayers that follow are designed as public prayers that elders or ministers could read at the communion table. Following the practice of the Christian Church (Disciples of Christ) and many other traditions, the prayers alternate between two prayers—one for the bread and one for the cup, or one for before and another for after communion—and a single prayer that can be read before communion. Each selection ends with notes for participation and often suggests a hymn from *Chalice Hymnal*.[4] Most of these hymns can be found in many other similar hymnals. All books, songs, and recordings mentioned in the meditations are cited in the bibliography. In the back is an index that lists the page numbers with the hymn titles and scripture references.

---

[4]*Chalice Hymnal* (St. Louis: Chalice Press, 1995).

These suggestions are meant to amplify whatever practice you have for celebrating communion. Many congregations say the words of institution prior to sharing in communion. They can be found in Mark 14:22–25 or 1 Corinthians 11:23–26. In some congregations, it is common for deacons to pass the bread and cup to the congregation. Sometimes the community eats the bread and drinks the cup as it is passed. More often the bread is eaten and the cup is held, and everyone drinks together as a sign of Christian unity. Another way to celebrate communion is to have participants walk up to the communion table, take a piece of bread, and dip it in the cup. If wine is used, you may also drink from a common cup and have an elder wipe the rim with a sterile cloth. You may have other practices in your community that would be included in the communion celebration. Whatever your congregation's practices are, the prayers in this book can help you focus during the time of communion.

This book may also be used in private devotion or group reflection. There are fifty-two entries so that you can read one a week for an entire year. The themes are listed in an order that suggests the celebration of communion. Chapters 1 and 2 begin with inner reflection; the next two chapters describe the reception of salvation; and chapters 5 and 6 complete our celebration with growth in faith and action. The sequence suggests that we confess our burdens and sins, celebrate God's saving grace in Christ and Mary, and are commissioned as ambassadors for Christ in the world. As a personal guide, my hope is that Roman Catholics and Protestants, seekers of faith, and those inspired by women mystics can use this book as a weekly devotion. An elder's group or study group might want to read a chapter a month and discuss each theme as it relates to their own lives of faith.

CHAPTER 1

Laying Down Our Burdens

Laying Down the Burden of Physical Illness

"But from the day of [my] birth, [I] was as it were entangled in a net of suffering and illnesses, so that [I] was vexed with continual pains in all [my] veins and flesh."

Hildegard of Bingen (in Petroff, p. 156)

Hildegard of Bingen suffered from debilitating headaches. Some think that the image of light that figures so prominently in her writings is actually a description of the blinding light of migraine headaches. Others wonder if her illness was caused by the stress of her difficult job as abbess of a large community of nuns. Hildegard herself thought that she was struck by illness because she refused to write down the amazing revelations she received from God. When she recognized her talents and began to write, she was able to get out of bed.

We are only now beginning to realize the complex relationship between our minds, our bodies, and the circumstances of our lives. Unfortunately this knowledge has not alleviated our pain; rather, it has increased the burden of physical illness. Whether we suffer from occasional headaches or chronic fatigue syndrome, we wonder what stresses have worn us down. If we suffer from arthritis or diabetes, we deal with the constant temptation to be defeated by our disease. When heart attack or cancer enters our lives, we are shocked by the reality of our own mortality. Even in this era of the Genome project, we suffer from physical illness and we share with Hildegard the need to lay this burden down before the One who is the Creator and Sustainer of life.

Communion Meditation

We come to this communion table with a multitude of physical ills. Whether our pains are minor or life threatening, they remind us of the limitations of our bodies. Whose pain do you bring to the communion table? Is it the pain of an elderly relative whose health melts before your eyes? Is it the injustice of a person in the prime of life stricken by cancer, heart disease, AIDS? Do you struggle with the crippling pain of a chronic disease or the aches and pains of aging?

Here at the table we are challenged by the witness of Hildegard of Bingen to acknowledge the physical ailments of our lives and lay them down before our Savior. This bread, which we break, is the bread that strengthens our bodies with the knowledge of the One who sustains us in the midst of pain. This cup, which we drink, is a reminder of the God-given energy for life that flows through our veins. Come and be nourished at the table of salvation.

Communion Prayer

O Great Physician, we come this day to lay down before you the physical burdens of our lives. Upon this table we place the fear, the anger, the frustration, and the agony of the pain in our bodies. We long for your healing touch and pray that this bread and this cup can be a medicine of consolation for our lives. We marvel at the memory of Jesus' healing ministry that reached out to the lame, the blind, and the bleeding. As he honored the bodies of all that he met, so we long to honor these bodies of ours and bring them before you in the hope of that healing Spirit that is gathered here in his name. In this bread, we remember his body, in this cup, we remember his life-giving blood. In this meal, we claim the hope of the resurrection of the dead. For it is in his name that we pray. Amen.

Suggestions for Celebration

Preparation: Place on the communion table an assortment of medicines and medical supplies. In the middle of the table, place the bread and the cup for communion.

Celebration: After reading the meditation, sing "These I Lay Down," verses one and five (*Chalice Hymnal,* # 391). Let each person take a moment to meditate on the pains in their lives. Share in a time of prayer in which each petition begins, "I lay down the burden of (name ailment or disease)," and all those present respond, "We lift this body to your healing care." Read the communion prayer and share in communion.

Laying Down the Burden of Mental Illness

"Whenever I was sick or depressed in my mind, the devil would begin to whisper that I would be damned."

Margery Kempe (p. 26)

The Book of Margery Kempe begins with a harrowing account of the anguish Margery felt after the birth of her first child. She had been ill throughout the whole pregnancy, and this had led to depression. Thinking she would die, she called for her confessor, who for some unknown reason interrupted her at the moment of her confession. Maybe he thought she was just a ranting woman; maybe he was too busy to wait for her to speak. Margery believed she would die and go to hell, which scared her to such an extent that she literally went mad.

It is heartbreaking to read how Margery tried to harm herself and others in her moment of desperation. What is worse is the fact that church officials did nothing to help her; rather, they made her problem worse. While she heard voices telling her that she was a worthless person, the church was silent. I wonder how different things are today? One of my friends told me that she knows a woman just like Margery. My guess is that we all do. Recent studies have shown that a large percentage of the United States population has admitted to bouts of depression. Like Margery, they hear voices that deny their intrinsic worth as a child of God. The table is the place to break the silence of their lives and replace it with the mercy of God's saving grace.

Communion Meditation

Voices surround this table. They are the voices of anguished men and women who are plagued by fear, despair, guilt, and depression. Accusations beat their spirits. "You are not good enough." "Your life has no future." "It doesn't matter anyway." "There is no way out of this." "Give up, give in, and get out." They are all lies, but they have the power to destroy life.

But this is the table of life, and here we hear the truth of salvation. "You are a child of God." "There is a room for you in the mansion of God." "You are the salt of the earth, the light of the world." "In Christ you are forgiven." "Come, follow him."

The medieval woman Margery Kempe was brought back from the valley of despair by the comforting words that Christ had not for one moment forsaken her. We stand in her company and know that no distress is beyond the presence of God. Come to the table and rest.

Communion Prayers

For the Bread: Gentle Shepherd, some days we stand in the valley of the shadow of death. We long for your guidance so that we might fear no evil. May this bread renew our courage, heal our despair, remind us of the promise that you abide with us always, and fill us with the knowledge that your rod and staff guide us toward our home with you. Amen.

For the Cup: May this drink, which represents the blood of life, remind us of the power of redemption to conquer the sorrow of the world. You prepare for us a table even in the midst of our enemies. As we drink of this cup of still water, may we be revived to see again your path of righteousness. May this communion time show us how to follow you to a pasture of restored spirits. Indeed, we thank you, for our cup overflows. Amen. *1-20-13 prayer*

Suggestions for Celebration

Preparation: Have the choir or a small group sing a version of the Twenty-third Psalm. One version that is very soothing is written by Lloyd Larson (GlorySound publication).

Celebration: Read the meditation and prayers for communion. Have the music of the Twenty-third Psalm playing in the background during communion. After the celebration, sing together "The Lord's Prayer" (*Chalice Hymnal,* #310).

Laying Down the Burden of Self-Hatred

"I looked at my body...I saw full well that it was my enemy."

Mechthild of Magdeburg (p. 143)

Like many medieval women, Mechthild of Magdeburg thought that it was necessary to hate her body in order to purify her soul. In this passage from her spiritual writings, she describes how she saw herself in conflict with her body. For twenty years she worked to conquer her body through fasting, scourging, and sleep deprivation. In her youth she cried in anguish from her inability to run fast enough to keep up with God. But in the end she had to confess that she remained needy in body and soul.

Although Christianity did not invent the idea that we are at war with our bodies, it is guilty of continuing a body-soul dualism that influences our society. The ever-increasing number of cases of eating disorders among young people is witness to the fact that this desperate battle for destructive self-control is still alive in our communities and our churches. Mechthild had the spiritual insight to realize that this was not God's will, and she came to understand that God supplied her every need, body and soul. Therefore, she should accept and honor her whole self as well. We, who are daily bombarded with images of bodily perfection, would be wise to follow the same advice.

Communion Meditation

In 1 Corinthians 12, Paul uses the analogy of a human body to describe the various members of a church community. A body has many parts, but it is made by God to work together as a harmonious whole. Therefore, all parts (and by analogy all members of the church) are necessary for the health of the whole body. We are so used to hearing the analogy that we forget the fact behind it. God has created us as bodily creatures that are in harmony only when we acknowledge the value of every member of the body. If one part suffers, we suffer entirely. If one part is hated, all are hated.

Like the medieval mystic Mechthild, we may need to confess the way in which the burden of self-hatred has brought suffering to our lives. By doing so we may be able to replace our destructive image with Paul's vision of our God-given bodies. Then we will come to the table able to rejoice in our body and spirit, to embody the unity that characterizes this communion, this community, and the church, and to witness to an eschatological banquet of wholeness for the world.

Communion Prayers

Before Communion: Holy Spirit, we come this day to be gathered in your loving arms, united in this community as one body. We confess the ways in which we struggle in our own lives for the same unity of body and soul. Like bread broken, our controlling spirits too often break our bodies. Like blood shed, our energy is wasted by our refusal to accept our talents and limitations. Forgive us, we pray, for this disregard of the goodness of creation. Here we witness to a body resurrected from death, blood poured out for the transformation of the world. Through this bread and this cup remold us into the Body of Christ. Amen.

After Communion: Gentle Spirit, in the breaking of this bread and the sharing of this cup, we have become one in the bond of love. Our hearts overflow with the mercy that fills our lives; our bodies rejoice in the care that sustains our lives. May we go forth ready to spread compassion and caring to the aching bodies of our world. Amen.

Suggestions for Celebration

Preparation: Read 1 Corinthians 12 and place on the communion table images or pictures of a foot, hand, ear, eye, and head. By the end of the reading, connect them together on a statue or outline of a body. Set it beside the bread and cup for communion.

Celebration: Read the communion meditation and prayer. As the communion is being passed, sing "One Bread, One Body" (*Chalice Hymnal,* #393). At the end of the song, rise and read the prayer after communion together.

Laying Down the Burden of Self-Doubt

"Ah, Lord Jesus, king of bliss, how shall I be comforted, who will tell me and teach me what I need to know, if I cannot at this time see it in you?"

Julian of Norwich (p. 267)

Julian of Norwich was a freethinker. While the church taught her that she was filled with sin, she could not understand how a loving God would create or judge her as blameworthy. It is hard for us to understand the degree of her distress. She was a dedicated Christian, loyal to the church and its teachings. She knew that to contradict official teaching could label her a heretic and endanger her life. Yet she also realized that to deny her own understanding of God's unconditional love could endanger her faith. Faced with such a difficult choice, she retired to a single room attached to a local church and spent her days in prayer, reflection, and worship. There she prayed the prayer above in her search for direction and comfort.

Even in our day of radical individualism, it is hard to be true to one's faith. We inherit a mixed set of messages about God and ourselves from our families, our culture, and our churches. In the book *Memories of God,* Roberta Bondi argues that we have to put down destructive images of God that burden our souls, and search for healing images that can help us recognize God's saving love and our own self-worth. Only then will we be able to overcome self-doubt. Years after her retreat, Julian was able to overcome her doubts and write down her revelations in a manner that held true to her convictions and added rich insight to our theological heritage. Her book, *Showings of Divine Love*, has helped generations of faithful Christians find God's love.

Communion Meditation

At this table we are confronted with the deepest mystery of our faith. How could God love the world in the face of the horror of the crucifixion? This meal reminds us of the depth of sin that causes death, destruction, and despair to the Son of God and the children of God throughout the ages. It confronts us with our own complicity with that evil, and the nagging feeling that we stand condemned, unworthy of God's love.

But this is not a table of guilt and judgment; it is a table of celebration. The body that we break is made whole in God's love, the blood that we shed rains down on the world in a realm of justice and peace. God's way is a way of reconciliation, a way of communion. An old hymn states that the love of God is broader than the measure of our mind. Come to the table for a taste of the redeeming love of God.

Communion Prayer

King of bliss, we gather at this table overwhelmed by the majesty of your love. Here we see the wideness of your mercy, a mercy that stretches to all ends of the earth through all generations and is made real to us in Jesus Christ. Through him we hear of a love that welcomes the stranger, that embraces the afflicted, that seeks reunion with the alienated, that is extended unconditionally to the world. In this meal, we participate in the nourishment of this message, and celebrate the victory of love that has the power to mend broken bodies and heal bleeding hearts. In gratitude we pray. Amen.

Suggestions for Celebration

Preparation: Sing "There's a Wideness in God's Mercy," verses one and two (*Chalice Hymnal*, #73).

Celebration: After singing the hymn, read the communion meditation and prayer. Share in communion. Join together in singing verses three and four of the same hymn.

Laying Down the Burden of Loneliness

"Lover, how can I do without you for so long?
Indeed, I am, alas, far too distant from you!"

Mechthild of Magdeburg (p. 300)

The life of a beguine must have been hard and lonely. Not only did Mechthild live much of her life without the companionship of a community of sisters or a husband and family, she often felt the pain of distance from God. Her life and ministry were fed by a profound religious experience of God's love. Yet in this poem, she laments the absence of this feeling of love in her life. Mechthild acknowledges that she cannot summon God at her command. No matter what her spiritual discipline or how many times she prays, the kind of mountaintop religious experience that feeds her soul is not something that she can produce at will. She writes that instead of an immediate answer to her prayer, God commands her to wait. Divine love is a gift that she can receive only in God's good time. And so, she turns to the lament of the psalmist to express the loneliness of her love for God.

There is no easy corollary between Mechthild's loneliness and our sense of loneliness. Few of us have severed all relationships to family and friends for the love of God. Most often we suffer the loneliness of being single in a couples-oriented society, of adjusting to an empty nest after years of child raising, or of grieving the loss of the love of our life. Maybe the best connection is just the experience of loneliness that is an element of all relationships. Mechthild reminds us that sometimes at the heart of our loneliness is the feeling of being abandoned even by God. To lament this reality is to give voice to our desire for communion and to bring that desire to God.

Communion Meditation

How many times have you come to this table hoping for some kind of experience of connection with God, only to have the bread turn to mush in your mouth and the sour taste of communion stick in your throat? In congregations that celebrate communion every time they gather, there is a danger of turning this sacred moment into a dry ritual, and the promise of communion into an experience of isolation.

This is a table of lamentation as well as celebration. The One who cried, "God, why have you forsaken me?" is at this table. In his cry is the anguish of the ages. It is here that we can confess the loss of our loved ones. This bread can nourish us through the pain of betrayal or unreturned affection. This cup can fill us with the strength to continue our search for communion. For it is here that we say we proclaim the Lord's death until he comes again. May we prepare ourselves for the coming of our Lord.

Communion Prayers

For the Bread: Love that will not let us go, we long to sense your presence in this communion hour. Come to us in this bread, symbol of your living body in the world. In this bread, we long to be filled with the comfort of your presence. Come quickly, Jesus, come. Amen.

For the Cup: Love that will not let us go, may this cup be a reminder to us of the sustenance that never forsakes the weary or the lost. May its sweet fragrance fill us with the memory of loves shared and pleasures enjoyed. May our thirst be quenched in this sharing of the cup of salvation, the promise of future love. For the love of Christ we pray. Amen.

Suggestions for Celebration

Preparation: Sing "O Love That Wilt Not Let Me Go" (*Chalice Hymnal,* #540).

Celebration: After reading the communion meditation, ask the congregation to meditate on those they love as an organist plays or a soloist hums an additional verse of the hymn. When the music is finished, invite participants to name aloud the loved ones that they bring to the communion table. Read the communion prayers and share in communion.

Laying Down the Burden of Betrayal

"She has very largely forgotten my affliction…She now leaves me in the lurch."

Hadewijch of Brabant (pp. 105, 106)

The words from this anguished letter written by Hadewijch of Brabant tell of the betrayal of one of her students, named Sara. It is hard to sketch out the details, but by reading between the lines of the letter it appears that Sara has left the beguine community or at least left Hadewijch's tutelage. Since beguines did not take vows of obedience, it was possible to leave a group to become married, return to one's family, or to join another community. We do not know what Sara did, just that Hadewijch misses her greatly and is shaken by her departure. Hadewijch does not condemn Sara for her actions and has to admit that Sara's love for God remains strong. It is just that her love for God does not translate into love for Hadewijch. Instead, Hadewijch writes, Sara is willing to let her suffer.

Betrayal by one we love is one of the greatest burdens of life. Loyalty is one of our most treasured possessions, and its loss causes hurt and anger that lead to fear and despair. Yet more and more we hear of loyalty betrayed by family members, institutions, religious leaders, and church communities. Even the cross is surrounded by the betrayal of Peter, of Judas, of the mob, of almost all the disciples. Yet Jesus is able to say, "Forgive them," and Hadewijch is able to write that she knows she will be reunited with Sara in heaven, if not on earth, because she is convinced that love is all. To hope for reconciliation is not a denial of betrayal's sting, but confidence that it too can be laid to rest in the bosom of God's love.

Communion Meditation

Troubling memories surround this communion celebration. The meal that was shared in the upper room is fractured by Jesus' prediction of desertion and is realized by Judas' kiss in the garden. Even Peter, the rock of the disciples, denies his loyalty before the morning dawns. The bread that we break is a recognition that the betrayal of that night is passed on through the ages in countless acts

22

of desertion. This drink that flows into the cup of communion is witness to the tears that we shed for lost hopes and broken dreams.

In the betrayals of our day, we have no idea how love and loyalty can be restored any more than we know how the medieval beguine Hadewijch survived the betrayal of her sister Sara. But we can follow her example and focus on the love of God that surrounds this table and draws into itself the burdens we lay down. We can remember that Peter is forgiven and able to be restored into the community of Christ by the love of God. Love *is* all. Come be restored in the people of God.

Communion Prayer

Lamb of God, we come to this altar of forgiving love to eat of this bread, symbol of your body made whole in our presence, and to drink of this cup as witnesses to the salvation offered to the world. At this table we lay down our grief and sorrow, our guilt and shame, and take up the vision of the reconciliation offered to us in Christ. Raise us up on eagle's wings; bear us on the breath of your new dawn. Amen.

Suggestions for Celebration

Preparation: After reading the communion meditation and prayer for communion, join in singing "What Wondrous Love Is This" (*Chalice Hymnal,* #200).

Celebration: Share communion. Then stand and sing "On Eagle's Wings" (*Chalice Hymnal,* #77).

Laying Down the Burden of Persecution

"Alas, dear Lord, almighty God, how long shall I stand here on the earth of my flesh like a stick or a target that people run, hurl, and shoot at, having long ago sullied my honor with cunning and malice?"

Mechthild of Magdeburg (p. 264)

It was not easy being a beguine. The idea of living free from family ties or church control challenged the social order of the medieval world. A free woman living a free life of service seemed dangerous if not heretical, so much so that church officials began to question their approval of beguines. At a synod in Mechthild's hometown of Magdeburg in 1261, beguines were ordered to obey parish priests. Mechthild does not tell us directly about this event, but she would have been in her fifties in 1261. Shortly after, she retired to a convent at Helfta to find refuge from the growing persecution.

While the era of the Inquisition is history, religious persecution continues to plague society. As religious diversity spreads in our communities, there is a temptation to lash out against new ideas and different perspectives. Litmus tests are on the increase in some denominations. In parts of our world, people still run, hurl, and shoot at each other in the name of their faith. Whether we have experienced persecution or read about it in the paper, we join Mechthild in asking, "How long, almighty God, how long?" God assures Mechthild that no one can destroy heaven; no one is swift enough, strong enough, cunning enough, or malicious enough to thwart God. The same hope lights our way.

Communion Meditation

How long, almighty God, how long? How long will we see crosses burning on church lawns? How long will we have to endure decrees condemning the ordination of women? How long will it be until we learn to build communities that welcome people of all religious faiths? How long will it take for us to learn from the history of the Inquisition, the condemnation of the beguines, and the horror of the Holocaust that God's way is not the way of violence, intimidation, and excommunication? We long for a time free from persecution for all your children.

At this table we hope for a glimpse of the banquet table that welcomes all and nourishes all with the bread and drink of salvation. Jesus showed us that the realm of God is an ever-expanding table that gathers all times, all places, and all peoples in the community of God. Let us come to this table to receive a foretaste of heaven and go from here to see the world anew from the perspective of what it can become.

Communion Prayer

Almighty God, we gather at your table this day hungry for the bread of heaven, thirsty for the cup of blessing. Here at this table we lay the names of those persecuted for their faith. We think of Christ, symbol of all those through the ages who have suffered for your love. We hear their cries of anguish. We mourn the wounds inflicted upon their bodies and spirits. We grieve the loss of life and liberty they have endured. We confess the ongoing persecution of our day and pray for your forgiveness. May this meal infuse us with the power of your justice, the strength of your endurance, the hope of your abiding love. For it is in the name of the One who triumphed o'er the cross that we pray. Amen.

Suggestions for Celebration

Preparation: Read aloud the quote from Mechthild. Ask participants to name aloud those persecuted for their faith. An alternative would be to ask participants to bring to the table place cards with the names of the persecuted, such as Jesus Christ, Perpetua, Mechthild of Magdeburg, and Oscar Romero. Read the communion meditation and prayer.

Celebration: Share communion. After communion, sing together "A Mighty Fortress Is Our God" (*Chalice Hymnal,* #65).

Laying Down the Burden of Conflict

"We are divided from one another in hatred and bitterness when we ought to be bound by ties of blazing divine charity."

Catherine of Siena (in letters edited by Noffke, p. 71)

There is nothing more disheartening than a church fight, and Catherine of Siena lived during one of the biggest fights in history. It is called the period of the Avignon papacy, the time during the fourteenth century when the pope was exiled from his home in Rome. For Catherine, a native of Italy, this rejection of her religious leader by factions in her own country was a scandal. Although she possessed no official power or status in the church, she worked diligently to mend divisions in the hope of getting the pope back to Rome. She wrote letters, chastised leaders, and gave a stirring speech to church leaders that inspired them into action. The letter quoted above is typical of Catherine's work. It is written to one of the ringleaders of the opposition, outlining the error of his ways and offering him reconciliation with the church. She closed this letter in her typical fashion with the hopeful words, "Gentle Jesus! Jesus love!"

We are no strangers to divisions in the church. The hostilities of the Reformation linger on in Northern Ireland. Many denominations are in danger of splitting over the issue of homosexuality. Local churches split over the choice of music, the role of ministerial leadership, or the color of the carpet. We can agree with Catherine that too often church members act like a bunch of "punyhearted fools." And maybe we can be inspired by her example to hold on to hope, to speak the truth, to keep our eyes on the possibility of reconciliation, and to trust that the unity of the Body of Christ is stronger than the divisions of the bodies that meet in his name.

Communion Meditation

There is a divine hospitality extended to us at this table. It is a place to put differences aside, to lay down the burden of division, to ask for guidance, and to open our hearts to the vastness and power of God's reconciling love. Paul reminds the church at Corinth that division profanes the body and blood of Christ. His words suggest that the unity offered at this table can only be realized when we examine our hearts and remember the hope of the One who prayed that we all might be one.

The bread that we share reminds us of all those who have worked for the unity of the Body of Christ. Here we meet Catherine of Siena, who worked for peace in the church at Rome. Here we pray for the leaders of the World Council of Churches and the National Council of Churches. Here we lift up those who work on discernment committees in various denominations. Here we celebrate those who work on local efforts for interreligious dialogue in our community. Here we remember the peacemakers in our own community. Here we drink together the cup, symbol of the life that connects us one to another in holy bonds of love.

Communion Prayer

Gentle Jesus, we gather in your presence this day to celebrate the memory of your redeeming work in the world. Help us to lift our eyes above the divisions that surround this table and gaze upon the one body that unites us all. May this bread strengthen us for the journey and this cup fill our mouths with the sweetness of your love. Gentle Jesus, Jesus love. Amen.

Suggestions for Celebration

Preparation: Read together 1 Corinthians 11:17–32. This could be followed by a discussion or homily on the meaning of this text for the community gathered to celebrate communion this day. Read the communion meditation and prayer.

Celebration: Share in communion. Afterward read Jesus' prayer for unity in John 17.

Laying Down the Burden of Oppression

"She's a woman. Why doesn't she stay in her cell, if it's God she wants to serve?"

From Raymond of Capua
The Life of Catherine of Siena (p. 339)

One of the biggest burdens of Catherine's life was the restriction placed on women of her era. As a young girl she felt called to a life of Christian service, but her family wanted her to get married. She battled with them for years before they accepted her vocation. This, however, was not the end of her troubles. She joined a group of laywomen noted for prayer and devotion. When she felt called to enter into the political battles of her day, her fellow sisters warned her that her action was unbecoming a maiden. To keep the peace, Catherine demanded that the pope write down his request for her to travel so that she could prove she had his blessing and avoid any scandal her actions might cause for her religious group.

Even in our day of growing opportunities for women, we are burdened by societal standards that oppress us all. Many Christian denominations restrict the roles of service open to women, and the most adamant proponents of the status quo are other women. More subtle forms of expectations limit opportunities for men. We box in ourselves and others with discrimination based on race, creed, and sexual orientation. Rising above these expectations takes courage, fortitude, and cunning. Catherine's strength came from her realization that in God there is no longer male or female. We are grateful that Catherine had the courage to get out of her cell, and we pray for the wisdom to break down the cells that surround our lives.

Communion Meditation

At this table we are offered a vision of a new realm where the powers and privileges of our day are laid aside for the opportunity to build a world of justice and harmony for all. In our increasingly separated society, here is a table where Jew and Greek, slave and free, male and female, are clothed in the unity of Christ. It is a place where we can lay to rest the restrictions that limit our lives and put on the mantle of the One who welcomes all to the table of redemption. May we be fed by the bread that unites us in one fellowship, and encouraged by the cup that empowers each of us to follow our unique call to Christian service. May this meal be a witness to a better world and a reminder of our power to light the world with the truth of justice for all.

Communion Prayers

For the Bread: Bread of Life, we hunger for a world of justice where all are nourished and all are fed. Yet we confess that we live where bread is broken, where privilege and oppression divide our communities, where lack of vision starves our souls. At this table we lay down the hateful remarks that bow us down, the prejudice that breaks our stride, and the discrimination that burdens our lives. May this bread sustain us in your love and give us strength for the journey to the table of unity offered in your name. Amen.

For the Cup: Living Vine, we drink this cup, symbol of the life that pulses through us and unites us as one people of God. May the sweetness of this drink fill us with the joy of redemption. May the memory of our Savior's shed blood remind us of the service that transforms the world. We celebrate you, risen friend, companion for our struggle, and guardian for our lives. Amen.

Suggestions for Celebration

Preparation: Begin by reading the quote about Catherine's life. Ask participants to confess discriminatory remarks that have burdened their lives. After each confession, have participants respond, "There is no longer Jew or Greek, there is no longer slave or free, there is no longer male and female; for all of you are one in Christ Jesus" (Galatians 3:28). Sing "An Upper Room Did Our Lord Prepare" (*Chalice Hymnal*, #385).

Celebration: Read the communion meditation and prayer. After communion, stand and sing "We Shall Overcome" (*Chalice Hymnal*, #630).

CHAPTER 2

Confessing Our Sins

Confessing the Sin of Self-Blame

"Sin is the sharpest scourge with which any chosen soul can be struck, which scourge belabours man or woman, and breaks a man, and purges him in his own sight so much that at times he thinks himself that he is not fit for anything but as it were to sink into hell."

Julian of Norwich (p. 244)

Julian had a unique perspective on sin. Rather than thinking we are too self-centered, she thought we were too filled with self-hatred and condemnation. In her mind, we spend too much time focusing on our failings and harboring the guilt that paralyzes our soul so that we conclude we are worthless, loveless, and doomed to eternal judgment. In another passage, she notes that the real problem with this perspective is that it makes God in our own image. The wrath of God is nothing other than our own projection of guilt. Julian reasons that wrath is not a divine trait, because it comes from lack of goodness, wisdom, and power, whereas God is by definition good, wise, and powerful. The way of God is the way of forgiveness; the path of faith is acceptance of this gift of grace.

When we scratch the surface of our self-assurance, we find layers of guilt and reprobation. Now, more than ever, people carry the burden of blaming themselves for not being good enough, smart enough, wise enough, or pure enough to measure up to God. We may even be misled by our religious upbringing to think that this way of confession is what God requires. One temptation is to turn inward and let blame consume our lives. A better option is to acknowledge our failings, offer them up to God, and rest in the assurance of never-ending love. Confession of sins is not an exercise in false humility; it is an active quest for acknowledging the truth of our identity as beloved of God.

Communion Meditation

In the parable of the prodigal son, Jesus reminds us that nothing can separate us from the love of God. Although the son expects punishment and condemnation, he receives honor and hospitality.

God, the always-forgiving father, rejoices in our presence at this table. In another parable, Jesus describes the vigilance of this hospitality as like that of a housekeeper who sweeps her home until she finds the one coin that has been lost. God sweeps Her world in search of the lost and forlorn.

We gather at this table mindful that the sages of the ages, from Julian of Norwich until today, have known of the power of the resurrection that is offered to us in this bread and this cup. Offered to us is the bread that makes us whole. Given for us is the cup that comforts our soul. Come to the table to receive the mighty gifts of God.

Communion Prayer

Forgiving Father, Merciful Mother, we come this day surrounded by the majesty of your love. At this table we confess the desire to run from your mercy and hide in the shame of our failures. We timidly eat this bread, hardly able to believe that in you we can be made whole. We cast our eyes from this cup, mindful of the blood that has been shed for our sakes. Yet the cup that we share is refreshment for our souls. Help us to share this meal confident in the assurance of your mercy, thankful for the new life of salvation. In your saving name we pray. Amen.

Suggestions for Celebration

Preparation: Prior to communion, read Luke 15:8–32. Read the communion meditation and prayer.

Celebration: During the sharing of communion, play "It Is Well with My Soul" (*Chalice Hymnal,* #561). After communion, sing the hymn together.

Confessing the Sin of Selfishness

"Then our Lord again complained and said: 'People drive me from the shelter of their heart with their selfishness, and when I find no room in them, I let them be in their selfishness.'"

Mechthild of Magdeburg (p. 286)

Mechthild struggled all her life with the temptation to shut out the love of God. Here she imagines Jesus as a pilgrim, searching the world for sinners. Jesus complains that some refuse to acknowledge him, others do not want him, and even Christians attack him. In anguish he tells Mechthild that people are trapped in their selfishness. Mechthild gives us a picture of Jesus as one who longs for our love, but knows that manipulation will not produce love. The sad truth is that love rejected is met by divine anguish. Yet even for those who have no room for him, Mechthild writes that Christ lights the way, in the hope that their hearts will return home.

We tend to think of selfishness as an act against other human beings, but here Mechthild reminds us that selfishness is shutting God out of our lives. It is denying the source of our being as a creature of God. To confess the sin of selfishness is to acknowledge the ways in which we forget this fact, the times we try to live as if we had no Creator, and the resistant spirit that shuts the love of God out of our lives. There is a letting go of the boundaries of our guarded souls that is required for the saving love of Jesus to enter into our lives. Making room in our hearts for this pilgrim begins with confessing our need, our acceptance, and our acknowledgment of that love.

Communion Meditation

At this communion meal, we are offered a vision of self-giving love in the body and blood of Jesus Christ. At Cana water flowed into wine as he provided for the wedding feast. On the hillside he fed multitudes with the bread of life and the message of salvation. To the woman who dared to touch his garment he gave his healing power. In the home of Zacchaeus he showed the world the gift of acceptance. At the news of Lazarus' death he wept. With everyone he met, Jesus opened his heart and offered the gift of salvation.

When he gathered his disciples in the upper room, Jesus took bread and broke it, reminding them of the ever-widening circle of God's love. He took wine and poured it in the cup, calling them to a life lived in unity with the love of God. His heart must have broken with the knowledge that one would betray that love. Yet his offer of a love that is freely given and freely received remains for them and for us the path of salvation. Come to the table and open your heart to the gift of self-giving love.

Communion Prayer

Loving God, we confess that too often we come to this table with guarded hearts, not ready to accept your hospitality, not willing to share in this meal of salvation. Our minds are so filled with our own passions and dreams that we forget it is you whom we meet here, you who long to enter our lives and make them whole. We confess the distractions that close our hearts. May this bread break open our resistance. May this cup pour upon us the mercy of your love. May this meal be for us the realization of coming home in the tenderness of your love. In the gentleness of your name we pray. Amen.

Suggestions for Celebration

Preparation: Read Matthew 11:28–30. Read together the communion meditation and prayer.

Celebration: Share in communion. Then sing "Softly and Tenderly" (*Chalice Hymnal,* #340).

Confessing the Sin of Anger

"Again, Alas! I regret the sinful tears that were shed in haughty anger."

Mechthild of Magdeburg (p. 278)

When Mechthild wrote these words, she had every reason to be angry. She had received so much criticism for her life of service that she had sought refuge in the convent at Helfta. Church officials had demanded that beguines be brought under the control of parish priests. Mechthild must have shed tears over the sad realization that her way of life was soon to be condemned, and with it all her life's work would be forgotten. Yet here she laments that anger did nothing to change things; rather, it consumed her strength and dried out her flesh. She likens anger to a worm that invades the heart and weakens its resolve. She confesses that the time wasted in anger was valuable time that could have been spent serving God.

The contemporary scholar Beverly Harrison has suggested that there is a power in anger because it is our body's way of telling us that there is something wrong. When we name it, we can work to eliminate the injustice that surrounds our lives. Yet too often we fail to acknowledge the problem and instead let the anger consume us. We may have been taught that anger is unchristian or uncivilized, and therefore we deny its existence. We may be too afraid or too powerless to change the situation. Mechthild speaks to us from the past, suggesting that we shed tears of sorrow and move on. After all, she was not forgotten, and her wisdom has been passed down through the ages to suggest to us that trust in God's patient justice can melt the anger that threatens our souls.

Communion Meditation

We have much to be angry at today. Our newspapers are filled with acts of violence in our community and throughout the world. Political leaders sacrifice the blood of the innocent for selfish gain. Even in the church we see the perpetuation of injustice acted out in Christ's name. Such blasphemy sickens our hearts and weakens our resolve. We confess that it is so easy to lose heart, so tempting to respond to violence with hatred, and so human to starve in the absence of righteousness.

At this table we call upon the wisdom of the ages and seek to be reminded of the great women and men of faith who have shed tears of anger for your sake. Like the women at the cross, we flinch at the cruelty of the world against the Son of God. We pray for the courage to wait patiently at your side for the glory of the resurrection. Here we celebrate the coming of your realm and witness to its power to transform the world and our lives. Here we come for the taste of justice that can nourish our souls.

Communion Prayers

Before Communion: God of grace and God of glory, at this table we place before you our anger and pray that in this meal we may receive strength for the journey and courage to face the path before us with honesty and hope. As we break this bread, we offer to you the brokenness of our hearts. As we drink this cup, we offer to you the sorrow of our lives. In the sharing of this meal, we pray for the healing of our hearts and the calming of our minds. In the power of your name we pray. Amen.

After Communion: God of grace and God of glory, we celebrate with you the salvation offered through our Lord, Jesus Christ. In the resurrection of his body we see the victory over the crosses of our lives. In the gathering of this community, we see the transformation of injustice into peace and love. Let us rise from this table filled with the joy of your new creation. Behold, the old has passed away and the new has come. Amen.

Suggestions for Celebration

Preparation: Sing together verses one and two of "Strong, Gentle Children" (*Chalice Hymnal,* #511). Read the communion meditation and give participants a moment for silent meditation.

Celebration: Read the communion prayers and share in communion. After the closing prayer, sing verse three of "Strong, Gentle Children."

Confessing the Sin of Neglect

"O you terribly foolish beguines, how can you be so insolent that you do not tremble before our almighty Judge, since you so frequently receive the Body of God out of blind habit."

Mechthild of Magdeburg (p. 121)

Even beguines were guilty of taking their faith for granted. Here Mechthild chastises her sisters for their casual observance of communion. For Mechthild, communion was the cornerstone of her religious life. It was in moments of communion that she experienced the saving love of God and received the strength to continue her life of service. She was fearful that her sisters had forgotten the mystery of salvation that sustained their lives. With neglect comes forgetfulness and weakened resolve. Earlier Mechthild had warned that humility without the fire of love ends in open hypocrisy. To reduce worship to a blind habit is to let the fire of love die in one's soul.

It is the regularly attending church members who are most in danger of letting the fire go out of their own worship experience. We often blame our lack of communion on others, charging that the music, the sermon, or the prayers did not awaken our spirit. The truth of the matter is that the presence of God is always there to greet us, especially in the communion meal. When we find ourselves counting the minutes until the service is over or planning the rest of our busy day, we have fallen into the same pattern of disrespect that plagued those foolish beguines. We need to guard against making this celebration so routine that it becomes devoid of emotion or expectation. Here we receive nothing less than the Body of God, a gift worthy of awe and adoration.

Communion Meditation

Each time we celebrate communion, we are offered the opportunity to meet our Savior face-to-face. Try to remember a time when your celebration of communion left you with the breathless wonder of meeting the living Christ. Were you sitting around a fire at church camp, or sitting in your hometown congregation? Did loved ones or a loving community of faith surround you? Did the taste of the cup fill you with the sweetness of salvation? Did the texture of the bread nourish you with the assurance of your faith? How long has it been since you came to the table filled with the knowledge that you are treading on holy ground? Come in expectation to the table of the Lord.

Communion Prayer

Almighty God, we tremble in the presence of this bread and this cup in anticipation of the salvation that is offered to us this day. We bow down before the majesty of this feast and the hospitality of this table. We are honored by the presence of such grace in our lives and humbled by your invitation to taste and see the goodness of your love. We are grateful for this community of faith that gathers in your name and for the boundless mercy that surrounds our lives. In our Savior's name we pray. Amen.

Suggestions for Celebration

Preparation: Prepare the communion table with colorful fabrics and beautiful adornments as if preparing for a feast or family gathering. After reading the communion meditation, have participants discuss memories of their favorite communion services. Encourage the group to share their joy in laughter, humor, and smiles. If someone suggests a special hymn, sing that together. Another choice is "I Come with Joy" (*Chalice Hymnal,* #420).

Celebration: Read the communion prayer. Share communion in a way that is meaningful for your community. You may come forward to the table to dip pieces of bread into a common cup or serve one another by passing the trays of bread and drink while singing your favorite communion songs.

Confessing the Sins of the Flesh

"I was almost constantly troubled with horrible temptations of the flesh and by despair."

Margery Kempe (p. 36)

Throughout her life, Margery struggled with sexual fantasies. In the fourth chapter of her autobiography, she recounts a three-year period when she was overcome with temptation and came close to committing adultery. The fact that she was married and had no interest in her husband compounded her shame. Reading about her uncontrollable desires is both shocking and yet uncomfortably familiar. She notes that everyone has some weakness and must constantly be on guard against giving in to temptation. The problem, she asserts, is thinking you can trust in yourself. Desires of the flesh remind us that misplaced trust leads to sin and heartache. The only remedy, Margery suggests, is confession, and reliance on the grace of God.

The church has never been very good at acknowledging that we are sexual creatures or honest about discussing the joys and dangers of physical desire. Certainly the mixed messages about virginity and motherhood that Margery received contributed to her problems. Today the church is out of touch with the temptations and possibilities that are presented to us. We read of people addicted to pornography and never consider that they may be sitting in our pews. We know that adultery and incest are present all around us, but we cover them with a silence of shame. Because of our refusal to be honest about our lives, we have repeated Margery's errors that led to denial, deception, and despair. We need to claim the courage to bring the struggles of her life and our own to communion with God.

Communion Meditation

At this table we celebrate a Savior who has authority over the demons of our lives. Because he is the Holy One of God, unclean spirits are silenced and people are made whole. This truth is not only the record of history; it is the living Spirit of God. We may be tempted to repeat the admission "What have you to do with us,

Jesus of Nazareth?" What does this table have to do with the temptations of our lives? How can the church help with the agony of adultery, the torture of temptation, the violation of abuse? Is there any way beyond silence, or shame, or self-destruction?

In Mark 1:21–28, a man with unclean spirits asks if Jesus has come to destroy him. Instead of retribution, Jesus silences his fears and exorcises his demons. The power that healed that man is present to us this day in the nurture of this community and the refreshment of forgiveness. Come to the table to feast on the bounty of God.

Communion Prayer

Holy One, we come to you today to celebrate the goodness of creation. Here we smell the fragrance of wholesome bread. Here we taste the sweetness of the fruit of the vine. The laughter of children fills our ears. The beauty of the human body delights our eye. The touch of loving friendship warms our souls.

At this table we lay down all that tarnishes the goodness of this creation in your image. We seek the cleanness of heart that comes through your mighty grace. We ask for the forgiveness of sin that renews our strength. We acknowledge the weakness of our lives and pray for your healing power, which makes us faithful, true, and whole. In our Savior's name we pray. Amen.

Suggestions for Celebration

Preparation: Read Mark 1:21–28. Meditate on the clean and unclean spirits of our lives. Sing or play "Silence, Frenzied, Unclean Spirit!" (*Chalice Hymnal,* #186).

Celebration: Read the communion meditation and prayer. As you share in communion, play the hymn slowly. At the end of communion, sing "Help Us Accept Each Other" (*Chalice Hymnal,* #487).

Confessing Sins against the Flesh

"I for my part don't know what else to do about it, except to beg you to ask supreme eternal Truth to grant me the grace of being able to eat."

Catherine of Siena
(in letters edited by Noffke, p. 79)

Catherine's well-known struggle with food is a sad chapter in the history of Christianity. During her youth she used fasting as a weapon to win control over her life. Eventually, her family relented to her desire to follow her own will. But she could not overcome her self-destructive habit. She was unable to eat in a normal manner the rest of her life. In this letter to one of her critics, she confesses that she forces herself to eat once or twice a day and prays continually for the grace to be able to eat. She asks her reader for advice and for the grace not to judge her too quickly. A few years later she died from a hunger fast at the age of thirty-three.

Like Margery, Catherine sees her behavior as a weakness that is based in an inappropriate form of self-reliance. Today we would diagnose Catherine as a victim of eating disorders that result from her desire to control her life. We can see how her family's expectations and the church's advocacy of ascetic practices contributed to her problem. And we can grieve that her self-destructive behavior is repeated today among people who are bright, talented, and struggling for control. We need to be on guard for the ways we punish ourselves for the frustrations of our lives. And we need to begin to honor our bodies as holy temples of the Spirit of God.

Communion Meditation

At this table we are reminded that we are members of the Body of Christ. The apostle Paul writes that our bodies are temples of the Holy Spirit, and as such they are to be honored. Just as we do not glory in Christ's body broken, but celebrate the transformation of that body in the resurrection, so we are not meant to break our bodies, but are called to witness to the power of God in the wholeness of our lives. Today we feast on the nourishment of this bread and give thanks for the food that sustains our lives. Here we relish the fellowship of the human community. We confess our need to overcome the extremes of feast and famine and pray for the balance that brings glory to God.

Communion Prayers

For the Bread: Living Bread, you are the source of all life. The bread that is broken at this table reminds us of the many ways that people struggle with broken bodies. As you were transformed from a body broken to a body reborn, so we pray for a wholeness of body and spirit redeemed in the Body of Christ. May this bread be for us the bread of new life. In the Body of our Risen Lord we pray. Amen.

For the Cup: Living Vine, you are the vine, and we are the branches that flow from the living water of your grace. In this drink we seek refreshment that can fill us with the living Spirit of your truth. Give us the wisdom to see ourselves as holy temples and the courage to ask for forgiveness for the ways we fail to honor our bodies. May this drink wash away our sin and remold us as members of the Body of Christ. Amen.

Suggestions for Celebration

Preparation: Read 1 Corinthians 6:15 and 6:20. Read the communion meditation. Ask the group to name aloud ways we break our bodies. Begin the time of confession by reading verse 15. End the confession by reading verse 20.

Celebration: Read the communion prayers. Sing verses one and two of "All Who Hunger, Gather Gladly" (*Chalice Hymnal,* #419). During communion, have a soloist sing "You Satisfy the Hungry Heart" (*Chalice Hymnal,* #429). After communion, sing verse three of "All Who Hunger, Gather Gladly."

Confessing Sins against Our Neighbors

"Those who choose injustice and hold it in their right and left hands are flattered by other people, but they do not listen to their masters or love the law or wish to serve the institutions of the law; all the things they do, they do only for themselves."

Hildegard of Bingen
(*The Book of the Rewards of Life*, p. 202)

Hildegard's writing is filled with vivid descriptions of the struggle between justice and injustice. At the heart of injustice is a disregard for one's neighbor. Cain commits the first act of injustice with the murder of his brother. Injustice stems from ignorance about our place in creation and a lack of understanding of the inter-connectedness of life. It is characterized by greed and a hardness of heart that Hildegard notes as the cause of great murders and minor vices. Hildegard is confident that God is at work in our world, defeating the forces of injustice and building a world of harmony and equity for all of creation. And we must choose to work with justice or be counted among the hard-hearted enemies of God.

It is hard to stand up against injustice. We are often ignorant about our place in creation. When we do open our eyes to the imbalance of the human community, we are paralyzed by the realization that we are benefactors of an unjust distribution of God's creation. The vice of greed keeps us from admitting the interconnectedness of life. Contentment with the status quo takes precedence over the law of God. To become aware of the world and confess our place in it is the beginning of justice. To stand up with the Hildegards of our day and work for justice is the beginning of communion with God.

Communion Meditation

Paul reminds the church at Corinth that all who eat and drink of the communion meal without "discerning the body" eat to their own condemnation. It is clear from his description that this discernment is not about the mystery of Christ's body but the injustice that exists in the Body of Christ. The table of communion is a table for the whole community, in fact, the whole world. At this table we share in God's plenty with all of creation. To close our eyes to the needs of our neighbors while satisfying our own thirst is unworthy of the vision of community that is at the heart of the realm of God. At this table we meet the visionaries of all days. Here we find Hildegard, who preached against greed and injustice. Here we sit with Martin Luther King, Jr., who had a dream of equality for all God's children. Here we find our host, our Savior Jesus Christ, who calls us to be a light to the world.

Communion Prayer

Flame of justice, we are gathered at this table as your community of faith. Here we are reminded that we must put aside our desire to be first in order to receive the nourishment offered in this communion meal. As we eat of abundance, we participate in the broken bread that fractures the world. As we drink of refreshment, we hear the voices of those who cry in thirst. Here we confess our desire to come to this table to satisfy our own hunger without regard for our neighbor's hunger and thirst. We pray that this meal will awaken us to the satisfying taste of your justice and light our way to the inbreaking of your realm. Amen.

Suggestions for Celebration

Preparation: Sing "We Are Not Our Own" (*Chalice Hymnal,* #689). Read the communion meditation.

Celebration: Read the communion prayer. Have participants serve one another the bread and cup of communion, saying, "This is the bread of life. This is the cup of salvation." After communion, read 1 Corinthians 11:27–33.

Confessing Sins against the Earth

"I will hang onto the beauty of this world as long as I can. I do not understand words spoken about another life when I have never seen it."

Hildegard of Bingen
(*The Book of the Rewards of Life,* p. 12)

The beauty of nature awed Hildegard. Her theology is filled with metaphors based on flowers and trees. In this excerpt from one of her writings, Hildegard describes a man who strips a tree bare of its flowers so that it dries up and falls to the ground. Hanging onto beauty means using and abusing the Earth without any regard for its future. It is both a sin against God's creation and a refusal to acknowledge the mortality of all of creation. The truth, Hildegard writes, is that the man, like the tree, will wither and die. To hang onto the Earth is a vain attempt to grasp immortality in earthly things. To care for the Earth as a fellow creature of God is the way of eternity.

The use and abuse of the Earth is one of the greatest sins of our age. Since most of us live so far removed from nature, we do not see how the habits of our lives damage the Earth. We adopt our culture's vision of the good life as a consumer life, a life that has earned the right to enjoy the fruits of our labor. Hildegard is correct in labeling the error of our ways. A true concern for the Earth must begin with the confession that we are not the center of the universe. We, along with all of creation, live and die in service to the glory of God. To make this confession is not to despair in the mortality of creation, but to enjoy life fully as stewards of the goodness of God.

Communion Meditation

At communion we enjoy the bounty of the Earth. We often hear that the elements remind us of the presence of the Divine. The bread is a symbol of Christ's body, and the drink reminds us of his blood. Have we ever thought about the presence of God in the symbols themselves? The bread that we eat is made from golden wheat that sways in the gentle breeze of the breath of God. The cup that we drink is full of purple grapes ripened in the warmth of God. We share this meal not only with Christians around the world, but with all of God's creation.

The apostle Paul writes that the whole creation groans for freedom from bondage. The salvation offered in Christ is the promise of redemption for the whole world. In Christ we celebrate not only the resurrection of our bodies but also the vision of a new creation. Here at this table we share a foretaste of the cosmic dimensions of the realm of God.

Communion Prayers

For the Bread: Creator of the Universe, we bow down before the beauty of your realm. We thank you for the abundance of creation and for our free use of the grains of the field. May the nourishment that we receive at this meal empower us to be the Body of Christ for the world. For it is in his name that we pray. Amen.

For the Cup: Creator of the Universe, we stand in awe of the fruitfulness of creation. We are reminded that we stand with the fruit of the vine in eager anticipation of the salvation of the world. We hear the groaning of the Earth as we shed its resources. As we share in this cup of salvation, may our sins against the Earth be washed away and our spirits renewed by the fruit of the Spirit. For it is in the Spirit of the One who is poured out for the world that we pray. Amen.

Suggestions for Celebration

Preparation: Fill the communion table with fruits, vegetables, nuts, and grains. In the middle of the table place the bread and drink for communion. Read Romans 8:18–25. Sing together verses one through three of "All Earth Is Waiting" (*Chalice Hymnal,* #139).

Celebration: Read the communion meditation and prayers. Share in communion. Following communion, sing verse four of the same hymn.

Confessing Sins against the Peoples of God

*"And yet in this I desired, so far as I dared, that I might have had
some sight of hell and of purgatory...But for all that I could wish,
I could see nothing at all."*

Julian of Norwich (p. 234)

One of the hardest things Julian had to confess was that she
could not believe in hell. She admits that it must be true because it
is a central teaching of the church, but it makes no sense to her.
Specifically, she wrestles with the final destiny of Jews who do not
convert to Christianity. Can those who reject salvation in Jesus Christ
still be saved? She knows that the church teaches they must be
condemned, but she cannot see it. In the end she resolves this conflict
between her beliefs and what she has been taught by suggesting that
we rejoice in the will of God. The more we fret about who is in or
out of hell, the further we will be from knowing the will of God.

Christian history is filled with judgment of the damned. Ever
since the establishment of Christianity as the official religion of the
empire, those who refused to convert to the true faith have been
judged as enemies of Christ. Christians have labeled Jews as Christ-
killers, pagans as goddess worshipers, and Muslims, Hindus, and
Buddhists as followers of false saviors. Even within Christianity those
teachings about Christ that were considered outside the norm were
declared heretical and their followers were burned at the stake. In
the face of such pressure to conform, it is rare to hear one such as
Julian struggle with the exclusivity of her faith. Her voice is timid,
and her final solution may seem evasive, but she is convinced that
the victory of salvation offered in Christ is universal, and she is
willing to trust in God's judgment about those who do not agree
with her faith.

Communion Meditation

How big is the table of communion? We often celebrate the
fact that it reaches across the world, joining together Christians of
all ages, races, times, and places. But what is the message of this table
for those who gather at other tables? What does this table teach us

about the Jews who gather for the Passover meal or the Muslims who celebrate the feast of Ramadan? For so many years we have shut our doors to those of other faiths that we have never considered setting a place for them as honored guests. The apostle Paul reminds us that in Christ, God has reconciled the world and given us the ministry of reconciliation. If we are truly ambassadors for Christ, our ministry will begin with a gracious hospitality that will trust in the victory of his love.

Communion Prayer

Almighty God, we are grateful for the hospitality that is offered at this meal. Here we receive bread of the world and wine of the soul. Yet we have hoarded this bread for ourselves and have erected barriers that keep us apart from other thirsty souls. Forgive us for our lack of hospitality and destructive vision. Fill us this day with a gracious spirit that welcomes our neighbor and provides hospitality to the stranger. Teach us how to be ambassadors of Christ and to trust in the power of his saving love. In his name we pray. Amen.

Suggestions for Celebration

Preparation: Read 2 Corinthians 5:16–20. Read the communion meditation. Ask participants to name aloud those who have been persecuted in the name of Christ. Then sing together "Bread of the World, in Mercy Broken" (*Chalice Hymnal,* #387).

Celebration: Read the communion prayer. Following communion, sing "In Christ There Is No East or West" (*Chalice Hymnal,* #687).

CHAPTER 3

*Celebrating
Our Savior*

Celebrating Christ as Food

"They have found table and food and waiter, and they taste this food through the teaching of Christ crucified, my only-begotten Son."

Catherine of Siena (*The Dialogue,* p. 145)

In Jesus Christ we celebrate the mystery of salvation. In this passage, Catherine imagines that mystery as the sustaining presence that strengthens our lives and fills our hearts with joy. She describes God as the table, food, and waiter of the Truth. Christ's teaching is the Word that satisfies our hunger. It is the food of life. And the table upon which this food is presented to us is the kindness of God, by which Catherine means that the foundation of salvation rests on the mercy of God. The Holy Spirit, who hears our needs and serves us the nourishment that fills our souls, offers this food to us. As table, food, and waiter, God sets for us a feast of salvation.

At communion we celebrate the central teaching of our faith. Like Catherine we should see this table as a welcome banquet that is set for us by the mercy of God. The idea of God as simultaneously the One who sets, serves, and is our salvation suggests to us that the presence and power of God work in many forms. At communion we can bring our joys and concerns to the One who hears our prayers and offers us guidance. Knowing that Catherine, who struggled with the inability to eat, describes Christ as food also suggests that communion is a time to hope for the strength to overcome all the obstacles of our lives. Here we find the food that fills our souls.

Communion Meditation

The gospel of John begins with the proclamation that in the beginning was the Word, and the Word was with God, and the Word was God. At this table we receive the hospitality of divine grace prepared for us from the beginning of the ages. In this bread and this drink we taste the living Word that strengthens us with the blessing of divine love. During this time of communion we are comforted by the knowledge that the Spirit hears our prayers and intercedes on our behalf with sighs too deep for words. (See Romans 8:26.)

Here we are offered the living presence of Christ. We hear the Word of salvation. We taste the food of forgiveness. We see the bounty of the goodness of God. Come with joy to the banquet of God.

Communion Prayers

Before Communion: Living Word, we come to this table filled with gratitude for the mystery of salvation. We come to proclaim the Word made flesh in our Savior Jesus Christ, who dwells among us this day in the sharing of the bread of life and the cup of salvation. As we eat of this bread, may we be nurtured by your words of comfort. As we drink of this cup, may we be refreshed by the power of your grace. In this meal, may we witness to the living presence of the Body of Christ. Amen.

After Communion: Light of the World, you shine upon this community in the sharing of this meal. As we are strengthened in your body and filled with your blood, may we shine to the world the word of saving grace. In our Savior's name we pray. Amen.

Suggestions for Celebration

Preparation: Set the table for communion with lavish china and the best linens. Make bread that is rich and wholesome and prepare a drink that is soothing and refreshing. Light a candle and place it in the center of the table. Read John 1:1–5 and then the communion meditation.

Celebration: If possible, have all participants gather around the table. Read the communion prayer. Sing together "Let Us Talents and Tongues Employ" (*Chalice Hymnal,* #422). Pass the bread and cup. Read together the prayer after communion.

Celebrating Christ as Bridge

"I made of him a bridge for you because the road to heaven had been destroyed."

Catherine of Siena (*The Dialogue*, p. 363)

The gospel of John proclaims that Jesus is the way, the truth, and the life (John 14:6). Catherine of Siena likens the way of Christ to a bridge that connects earth to heaven and us to God. To imagine the saving work of Jesus as a bridge suggests that he forges a path for faithful living. Catherine calls this the life of grace because the example of Jesus is a gift from God. But salvation is more than a road map through life's stormy waters; it is the key that unlocks the pathway to God. God gives us Christ, who bridges across the sin that blocks our journey, provides for us a foundation of love that supports our steps, and accompanies us with the lantern of peace to light our way. Through Christ we come home to God.

Communion is the celebration of the bridge between heaven and earth. Catherine writes that Christ is the meeting of the human and the divine. As his arms stretch across the cosmos, we are united with the love of God. She writes that Christ's blood is mixed with his divinity in burning love for our salvation. Likewise, our humanity is kneaded with his divinity in communion with God. Through the mystery of salvation we come home to our true selves as created in the image of God. We come to communion confident that we walk with Christ, in Christ, and through Christ on the pathway of salvation.

Communion Meditation

There is an old saying that any journey begins with a single step. Today we celebrate that the journey of communion began with the step of our Savior, whose life, death, and resurrection forged for us a pathway to God. In the wisdom of his teaching we learn the truth about the saving love of God. In the witness of his living we see the justice of the reign of God. In the suffering of the crucifixion we acknowledge the compassion of the way of God. In the victory of the resurrection we celebrate the power of salvation that bridges the journey from death to life, sin to salvation, us to God. As we come to this hour of communion, let us lay aside all that hinders our journey and partake of the food that strengthens our step and guides our way.

Communion Prayer

Rock of salvation, we celebrate the path that is set before us in the body and blood of Jesus Christ. The bread that unites the world in faith reminds us of Christ's body stretched from heaven to earth to sustain us in saving love. The cup that quenches our thirst refreshes us with the good news of saving grace that guides us along the path of righteousness. As we eat this bread and drink this cup, we commit ourselves anew to the way of truth, the life of faith, and the path of justice. For it is in the name of the One who leads us all the way that we pray. Amen.

Suggestions for Celebration

Preparation: Sing together "All the Way My Savior Leads Me" (*Chalice Hymnal,* #559).

Celebration: Read the communion meditation and prayer. During the sharing of communion, play "Bridge Over Troubled Water" by Paul Simon and Art Garfunkel. After communion, sing together "O Christ, the Way, the Truth, the Life" (*Chalice Hymnal,* #432).

Celebrating Christ as Gardener

"He was to be a gardener, digging and ditching and sweating and turning the soil over and over, and to dig deep down, and to water the plants at the proper time."

Julian of Norwich (p. 273)

Julian describes Christ as a gardener who tends the harvest of salvation. In coming to Earth, Jesus begins the work of cultivating the world to grow in the fullness of God. Gardening is hard work that requires blood, sweat, and tears. The constant tending of the harvest demands patience and perseverance, as well as the wisdom to know when to nourish plants with water and when to let them grow in the sun. Like all gardeners, Jesus rejoices in the bountiful harvest. Then he offers the fruits of his labor to his master. The culmination of his work is to return the bounty of the earth to its maker so that the dust of the earth fulfills its destiny to give glory to God.

This earthy description of the work of Christ suggests that salvation is a process of cultivation. We are the fruit of creation that needs to be warmed by the rays of divine love and nourished by the waters of redemption. Our growth is placed in the confident hands of the Master Gardener. As roses that bloom in the gardens of summer and as wheat that sways in golden fields, we reach our fullest potential when we blossom with the love of God. The life, death, and resurrection of Jesus are part of this work, and the harvest is the resurrection of our bodies in the realm of God.

Communion Meditation

One of Jesus' best-loved parables is that of the mustard seed that grows from a tiny seed to a large tree that provides refuge for the birds of the air. Have you ever thought of yourself as a seed in the realm of God? Such an image reminds us of our status as part of God's good creation. It also suggests that we are to grow in the life of faith to be a blessing to others. As the grain of the field, we can become the bread of life for another. As the fruit of the vine, we can bring refreshment to creatures of the earth. As flowers of the garden, we can grow in beauty and strength to adorn the realm of God.

Of course, our growth depends on the One who waters and prunes our lives. Julian of Norwich writes that Christ is the gardener of our souls. We rejoice in the way he has prepared the field of salvation by digging up the stones of rejection from the earth and planting the seeds of forgiveness in the hearts of humanity. As we come to this meal, we wait for his expert touch to prune the imperfections from our souls and to shape our lives to bloom in beauty and grace.

Communion Prayer

Creator of the Universe, as we gather at this harvest table, we see the goodness of creation prepared for us in bread and wine. Cleansed in the waters of baptism, we come to this table ready to partake in the bounty of salvation. As we eat this bread, we are nourished in the presence of the living Christ who strengthens our spirits. As we drink of this cup, we are filled with the power of the living Christ who turns over all that hinders our souls. Melt us, mold us, fill us, use us, to the glory of your name. Amen.

Suggestions for Celebration

Preparation: Fill the communion table with fruits, flowers, and grains. Place the bread and cup in the middle of the table. Sing together "Sheaves of Summer" (*Chalice Hymnal,* #396).

Celebration: Read the communion meditation and prayer. During communion, sing "Spirit of the Living God" (*Chalice Hymnal,* #259). After communion, read the parables of the mustard seed and leaven found in Luke 13:18–21.

Celebrating Christ as Fellow Sufferer

"I bore my cross with them; when they are downcast, they should remember me."

Mechthild of Magdeburg (p. 322)

When Mechthild felt imprisoned in the difficulties of her religious community, she prayed for words of comfort. What she received was a reminder of the many ways in which Christ is present with those who suffer. What follows is a list of events from the life of Jesus and the life of her community in which over and over Christ says, "I was with them." Such knowledge not only gives her the courage to face suffering but to know that she does not suffer alone. Because Christ has fasted in the desert, been tempted by the enemy, and borne the cross, Mechthild gains confidence that she too will endure being taken into court, persecuted for her beliefs, and faced with death. Because Christ arose from the dead and ascended into heaven, she knows that through Christ she will rise out of her suffering. As Christ entrusted his Spirit to his Father, so she entrusts her spirit to Christ.

The Middle Ages was a time that celebrated the humanity of Jesus. In an age when God was imagined as a distant power that ruled over and judged the earth, salvation came in the news that Jesus walked this earth and communed with the faithful as a fellow traveler. The power of God is not a power over our lives, but a present power that lives in, with, and through us so that we can be freed from all that imprisons our lives. The message of the cross is not that suffering saves us, but that there is a divine presence that saves our suffering.

Communion Meditation

In moments of suffering there is no greater gift than the gift of presence. To sit with a friend in time of sickness or to visit the bereaved is more powerful than all the medicine in the world. Likewise, the gift of salvation is a gift of presence. We celebrate a Savior who teaches on the hillside, eats in people's homes, heals with his touch, and cries with his friends. In the symbols of bread and drink, we claim anew that Jesus is named Emmanuel, God with us.

Today we celebrate the fact that the One who walked the earth two thousand years ago abides with us in this community of faith. In this community, we gather around a table to share a meal, hear the words of salvation, receive the healing nourishment of bread and wine, and share together the laughter and tears that fill our lives. We are united in the promise of the One who proclaimed, "And remember, I am with you always, to the end of the age" (Matthew 28:20).

Communion Prayer

Precious Savior, at this table we come seeking the sustenance of your abiding presence. At your feet we place the pains of our bodies and the burdens of our souls. To your listening ear we confess the temptations that torment our hearts. In your care we leave the sufferings of our lives and the divisions in our community. Within sight of your watchful eye we lift up the inequalities of our world. You stand with us in the wilderness. You walk with us through the desert. Even in the shedding of blood and the breaking of bodies you abide. We rest in the solace of your promise to be with us always. In the name of the One we dare to name our friend we pray. Amen.

Suggestions for Celebration

Preparation: Read the communion meditation. Meditate on the places in your life and the world where the presence of Christ is needed. Sing together "What a Friend We Have in Jesus" (*Chalice Hymnal,* #585). After the hymn, name aloud your concerns. End each petition with the phrase "I take it to the Lord in prayer."

Celebration: Read the communion prayer. As you share in communion sing the hymn "Lo, I Am with You" (*Chalice Hymnal,* #430). As you sing the last verse take the elements off the communion table and carry them out of the sanctuary.

Celebrating Christ as Mother

"Our savior is our true Mother, in whom we are endlessly born and out of whom we shall never come."

Julian of Norwich (p. 292)

As Julian is grasping for a way to describe the unconditional love of God in Christ, she suggests that Christ is our Mother. In Christ we celebrate the unconditional love of one who bears all things, endures all things, and hopes all things for our salvation. As a mother feeds her children, so Christ feeds us on the bread and wine of communion. Like a mother who works for the welfare of her children, Christ nurtures and guides us as we grow in stature and faith. With a mother's courage and determination, Christ bears us in the pain of the crucifixion so that we can be born in new life.

It may be shocking for us to discover that this feminine image of Christ is presented in writing that dates back to the 1400s. To think of Christ as our mother gives us fresh language and new insight into the mystery of salvation. To be born in Christ suggests that the pain and suffering of the crucifixion are the birth pains of salvation. The blood of Christ is the spilling forth of the womb of God. As we are baptized, we are born into newness of life through the birthing waters of baptism. As we share in the bread of communion we celebrate the manifold ways in which the Body of Christ nurtures us. Even in our most unsightly moments we find consolation in the bosom of our savior. In communion we come home to the embracing arms of God.

Communion Meditation

The idea of motherhood elicits a wide array of responses from any community. Some people have feelings of warmth, security, and gratitude. Others react in fear, frustration, and anger. To suggest that Christ is our mother may likewise comfort some and upset others. Julian of Norwich said that regardless of our own experience of motherhood, to name Christ as our mother is to trust in the perfect love of God.

So what does it mean to name Christ as our Mother? How could this image bring fresh understanding to your life of faith? Do you seek in God a place to rest and be comforted? Are you at a stage in your life when you need to be reborn? Are the pains that you are called to bear part of the birthing of the realm of God? As you think upon these things, come to the table to claim your identity as the beloved child of God.

Communion Prayers

For the Bread: Mother Jesus, we come to this table weary from our labors to rest in the bosom of your endless love. In this bread we seek the nourishment that will sustain our lives. We pray that in this communion hour you will fold us in your arms and lavish your care on us. We come to seek the wisdom of your grace and to be fed by the truth of your Word. As your grateful children we pray. Amen.

For the Cup: Womb of life, we stand at this table, hearts filled with gratitude for the gift of life. In the waters of creation you shaped the earth. In the waters of Mary you gave birth to the promise of salvation. We see that promise fulfilled in the water that poured forth from our Savior's side. In this cup we are reminded of the life-giving power that pours upon us each day. We pray that this meal will refresh us with newness of life so that we might overflow with your mercy. Amen.

Suggestions for Celebration

Preparation: Share in a Bible study of feminine images of God. Sing together "Mothering God, You Gave Me Birth" (*Chalice Hymnal,* #83).

Celebration: Read the communion meditation and prayers. During communion, think about what it means for you to call Jesus your mother. After communion, share your reflections with the group.

Celebrating Christ as Nurse

"My son was your wet nurse, and he joined the bigness and strength of his divinity with your nature to drink the bitter medicine of his painful death on the cross so that he might heal and give life to you who were babies weakened by sin."

Catherine of Siena (*The Dialogue,* p. 52)

This image of Christ as wet nurse of our salvation shares Julian's feminine imagery of being fed by Christ, but for Catherine the feeding is not just the food that nurtures our life of faith but the vehicle for healing us from sin. Her analogy is based on the practice of transmitting needed medicine to infants through breast milk. If given to the baby directly, the medicine will kill the child. The wet nurse, however, can take the medicine without repercussions and pass it on to the child in her milk. The crucifixion is the medicine for our salvation. Since Jesus is of God, death does not defeat him, but is able to be transformed by him into the eternal life that heals our souls.

It is not unusual to think of sin as a disease that threatens our life. Not only do we know about the relation between spiritual and physical health, we can resonate with the fact that sin invades our lives and takes us over in a way that we cannot overcome. If sin is like disease, the corresponding remedy should be medicine, not punishment. Cancer patients are not healed by judgment, but by effective medicine and treatment. Likewise, we need to be healed from our sin.

It is unusual to consider the crucifixion as the medicine of salvation. A donor might give blood to save another life, but can the crucifixion be considered the blood transfusion that saves our lives? Catherine's suggestion is certainly unorthodox, but it does give us a new way to consider how we benefit from the sacrifice of Christ. We affirm that his sacrifice is life-giving rather than life denying, because Christ is not defeated by the crucifixion. And we rejoice that in this life-giving act we are restored to health.

Communion Meditation

What does it mean to consider Christ the nursemaid of our salvation? Catherine of Siena thinks of Christ as the great doctor of our faith, able to heal the sin that infects our souls through taking the sin of our lives into his own body and overcoming it so that we might be restored to health. We often gather at this table and speak of the body broken and the blood shed for our sins. But too often we focus on his suffering as a punishment for our sins rather than as a means for our redemption. We celebrate the resurrection as the cure, the crucifixion as the treatment, and Christ as the wet nurse of our salvation. We come to this table to celebrate the life-giving blood that makes us whole.

Communion Prayer

O Great Physician, you have made us from the dust of the earth and have restored us with the blood of salvation. Your healing touch has cured the sting of death with the hope of eternal life. In the body and blood of our Savior, Jesus Christ, we celebrate the mystery of your healing powers. In this bread and this cup we join with the rest of creation in the renewal of the world to the glory of your realm. In the name of the healing One we pray. Amen.

Suggestions for Celebration

Preparation: Read 1 Peter 2:24. Read the communion meditation. Sing together "The Blood Will Never Lose Its Power" (*Chalice Hymnal,* #206).

Celebration: Read the communion prayer. During communion, play or hum "There Is a Balm in Gilead" (*Chalice Hymnal,* #501). After communion, offer a prayer for healing. For an example, see *Chalice Hymnal,* #505.

Celebrating Christ as Child

"Take me as your dear darling, as your sweet son; I want to be loved as a son should be loved by his mother."

Margery Kempe (p. 133)

Julian likens the unconditional love of God in Christ to a mother's love. Margery Kempe reverses the imagery to imagine the vulnerability of that love as a childlike love. Jesus, born in Bethlehem, shows us that God does not come into our midst as a coercive power demanding our love, but as a helpless child who needs our love and care. Since much of Margery's life had been a struggle with her own identity as a mother, this invitation to think of Jesus as her child helps her to realize that God accepts her as she is. She does not have to set aside her earthly loves in order to love God, but is called to love God with motherly devotion and care. For Margery this revelation is saving grace.

We are so used to identifying the crucifixion as the saving event of Jesus' life that we forget the importance of the incarnation as the indwelling of God's presence in human form. Like Margery we need to take a moment to reflect on the importance of Jesus as one who comes to us as a little child. To think of Jesus as a little child breaks all our illusions about God's saving power as a dominating force. Children need us and trust in our loving care. They also present us with joy for life and hope for the future. In the little child born in Bethlehem we catch a glimpse of our salvation.

Communion Meditation

During Advent we think of the mystery of God coming to us in the form of an innocent child. The Christmas story is filled with the news of Jesus' humble status. He is born in a manger, not a castle; he grows up in Nazareth, not Jerusalem; and he is trained as a carpenter, not a king. Yet shepherds from hillsides nearby and rulers from faraway lands recognize him as Emmanuel, God with us. Simeon did not have to wait to see Jesus' miracles, hear his teachings, or witness the crucifixion in order to know that in this infant was the salvation of the world. We who come to the communion table are invited to recognize our Savior in the form of an infant. As a child he comes into our hearts, awakening in us a tender and adoring love. Here we hold the body of the babe who is our hope and our future.

Communion Prayer

Infant holy, infant lowly, we join with the voices throughout the ages to proclaim that Christ the babe is born for us. Like Simeon we see in this little body the light of revelation and the presence of God. With Anna we proclaim the life of this little one to all who are looking for redemption. We come to this table with hearts overflowing with gratitude for the miracle of new life and bursting with joy for the bright future that awaits us all. Open our hearts to the wonder of your grace and the presence of your love. In the name of the babe of Bethlehem we pray. Amen.

Suggestions for Celebration

Preparation: During Advent and Christmas, symbols of the season, such as a nativity set, may be placed on the communion table. Other times of the year you may place on the table pictures of babies or pictures of Jesus drawn by small children. If your congregation has the practice of placing a rose in the sanctuary when there is a new birth, consider placing a rose on the communion table to celebrate Jesus' birth. Read Luke 2:25-38. For a hymn of preparation sing "like a child" (*Chalice Hymnal,* #133).

Celebration: Read the communion meditation and prayer. After communion, sing together "Infant Holy, Infant Lowly" (*Chalice Hymnal,* #163).

Celebrating Christ as Lover

"I must go from all things to God, Who is my Father by nature, My Brother by his humanity, My Bridegroom by Love, And I his bride from all eternity."

Mechthild of Magdeburg (p. 61)

Mechthild's poetry is filled with descriptions of Christ as the lover of her soul. Her words paint a graphic picture of the joys and frustrations of being in love with Christ. She longs for the love of Christ, is often impatient with anything that keeps her away from her lover, and strives to live a life worthy of his love. In return Christ is one who desires her love, comes to her in moments of prayer and meditation, and fills her life with joy. She celebrates a love that surpasses all human limits and offers her the heights and depths of union with God.

The idea of Christ as our lover shocks our imagination. There is something too human and irreverent about this notion that the love of God could be romantic, passionate, or erotic. Few of us would want a love that is so exclusive or so demanding. And certainly, the beguines were an unusual group. They sought a form of Christian life that was all consuming and were willing to risk ridicule and persecution for the opportunity to love God freely. What beguines like Mechthild teach us is that the love of God is endless. The love of God can satisfy the deepest longings of our souls. No love is stronger and no love can promise more. We just need to have the imagination and the courage to ask.

Communion Meditation

One of the first songs we learn as a child is "Jesus Loves Me." The chorus can bring a smile to our faces and fill our imaginations with childlike devotion. But the love that satisfies us as children is not enough to express the longing of our grown-up desires. Throughout history Christian mystics have challenged us with the idea that God's love satisfies the deepest passions of our souls. Jesus himself reminds his followers that they are not only children of God, servants of the Master, but friends and lovers of the Son of God.

At the communion table we celebrate the greatest of loves. Jesus proclaims that we are called to be friends of God and lovers of the world. Do we come to this table expecting little from these mere morsels of bread and drink? Or do we come expecting this bread to satisfy our deepest longings and this cup to quench our spiritual thirsts? At this table we are offered the abundance of God's love in the body and blood of our Savior Jesus Christ. Why do we settle for mere appearances of God's love when we are given the opportunity to taste the fullness of love in bodily form? We have been chosen and we are called to take our place at the table as the beloved friends of God.

Communion Prayer

Jesus, lover of our souls, we come to you at this communion table to taste and see the goodness of your love. We confess that we are tempted to run away from a love so profound that it invades the depths of our souls. We ask for your mercy to wash over us with forgiveness for our timid hearts. We pray that as we eat this bread we will be filled with the passion of your love. When we drink this cup may we be enflamed with the justice of your love. In all that we do may we celebrate the magnitude of our calling as the friends of God. In the name of the One who has chosen us we pray. Amen.

Suggestions for Celebration

Preparation: Read John 15:12–17. Sing together "Jesus, Lover of My Soul" (*Chalice Hymnal* #542).

Celebration: Read the communion meditation and prayer. During communion, play familiar love songs or read passages from the Song of Solomon.

Celebrating Christ as Light

"And you see a serene Man coming forth from this radiant dawn,
Who pours out His brightness into the darkness."

Hildegard of Bingen (*Scivias*, p. 154)

Hildegard had a unique way of envisioning the mysteries of salvation. Her writing is filled with natural images that depict the work of God. In a picture entitled "The Redeemer" she draws Christ as a figure of pure light that breaks into the darkness that encases humanity. With one touch, humanity is enflamed with Christ's light and rises out of darkness to the light of new day. Each person becomes a star that shines in the darkness of the world, until finally the whole cosmos is ablaze with the shining light of divine glory.

We are so accustomed to thinking of Christ as our personal Savior that we neglect the cosmic dimensions of his saving work. Hildegard reminds us that the work of Christ is more than a personal relationship; it is a force of spontaneous combustion that seeks to overcome all the darkness of creation. When Christ touches us, we are literally enlightened to shine forth with his mercy and justice in the world. His incarnation is the breaking forth of the light of salvation in the world, and we are the light of the world.

Communion Meditation

One of the most moving services of the year is the candlelight service on Christmas Eve. During the darkness of winter, one candle is lit to represent the inbreaking of the light of God in Christ. Slowly the light is passed from one to another until the whole sanctuary is ablaze in the soft glow of candlelight. The atmosphere is filled with peace and goodwill, and for a moment all is right with the world. I remember leaving the sanctuary on one special Christmas to be greeted by the freshness of newly fallen snow. As the organ rang out the chorus to "Joy to the World" I looked to see the whole world aglow with the beauty of redemption.

At the communion table every day is Christmas day. The light of the world is offered to us in Christ's body. This bread and this cup remind us of the One who came into our midst to light a path for our salvation. His light continues to burn around this communion table and throughout the earth whenever the good news is proclaimed. Let us come to be filled with the light of salvation so that we might shine forth with his truth and righteousness.

Communion Prayer

O Morning Star, you shine upon us with the goodness of creation and the redemption of salvation. As a star in the east you lead us to salvation. As a light shining in the darkness you search out the lost until all are returned to the warm glow of your grace. We rejoice in the light of your grace that beams in our midst and encircles this table in your love. We join with friends and neighbors in the presence of angels and all of creation to shine forth in the light of your redemption. Amen.

Suggestions for Celebration

Preparation: Light a Christ candle on the communion table and surround it with candles of various sizes and shapes. In the middle, place the communion bread and cup. Read John 1:4–5 and Luke 15:8–10. Read the communion meditation and sing together "O Morning Star" (*Chalice Hymnal,* #105).

Celebration: Read the communion prayer. Ask each person to come forward to share in communion. After eating the bread and drinking the cup, take a candle, light it, and return to your seat in the congregation. After communion, sing together "Joy to the World" (*Chalice Hymnal,* #143).

CHAPTER 4

Standing with Our Sister Mary

Standing with Mary as Fellow Mourner

"Deep within my soul, I thought of our Lady, how she had mourned and shed tears when her son had died. I felt I shared all her sorrows as my own."

Margery Kempe (p. 109)

For Margery, the story of Jesus was not just a past event; it was a present reality that she relived each year. She imagined each event of Jesus' life in vivid detail, imagined what it would be like to be in his company, to live with his followers, and to know his companions. Of all his followers, she most identified with Mary. She could see how Mary worried about her child, how she would care for him with loving devotion, and how she stood vigil at his side during his time of suffering. As she imagined Mary's grief, Margery would be overcome with sorrow for the suffering of Christ. She could see herself standing at the cross with Mary, overcome with pity for Mary's loss and with compassion for the suffering of the world. In solidarity with her sister Mary, she wept for the sins of the world.

There is no doubt that Margery was a religious fanatic. Her weeping was a constant source of irritation for religious leaders. When asked to stop crying, Margery replied that Christ's death was as real to her as if it had happened that day, and so, she thought, should it be for every Christian. Margery not only believed in the mystery of salvation; she felt it. In feeling the pain of the crucifixion she opened herself up to the sorrow of the world. Like Mary, she tried to care for those who suffered and endured pain. Fanatic or not, Margery challenges us not only to believe in, but to feel the gospel, and to live it out in each day of our lives.

Communion Meditation

We come to the communion table so frequently that we are immune to the pain and suffering that we remember here. How glibly we remember Christ's broken body and shed blood without any feeling for the pain and sorrow of his death. Maybe it is time to remind ourselves of the agony of those days. How would it have been to stand at the cross of Christ, knowing him not only as our

Savior but also as our teacher, our brother, our son? At the cross of Christ stands his mother, Mary, and in the sorrow that sweeps over her soul we can witness the heights of loving devotion and the depths of helpless despair.

Do we come to the table with the same overwhelming feeling that the pain of the world is beyond our control? Then here we can take solace in the witness of our ancestors. Like Mary, we do not have to run away or hide our faces. With courage and quiet strength we can stand at this table and mourn for the suffering that overwhelms our lives, damages our communities, and invades our world. With Mary we mourn, and we wait for the resurrection of the world.

Communion Prayer

Almighty God, we pray for strength to come to this table and face the horror of suffering and death. We remember the agony of your Son, who endured the cross for the redemption of the world. We mourn the loss of one so pure, so good, so compassionate, so divine. Why is it that the beautiful and the lovely are struck down by the evil of the world? Why are the courageous and the compassionate in everyday life so often defeated? At the foot of the cross we stand with those who first endured the loss of our Savior. And we wait patiently for your strength and your power to reign victorious. Come quickly, Lord Jesus, come. Amen.

Suggestions for Celebration

Preparation: Place a cross on the communion table and drape it with black cloth. Set flowers at its base and the bread and cup of communion by its side. Read Mark 15:33–41. Read the communion meditation. Sing together "Were You There" (*Chalice Hymnal,* #198).

Celebration: Read the communion prayer. During the sharing of communion, sing "Sing of Mary, Pure and Lowly" (*Chalice Hymnal,* #184). After communion, read Luke 2:14–19.

Standing with Mary as Virgin Bride

"The Father chose [Mary] for his bride—that he might have something to love; for his darling bride, the noble soul, was dead."

Mechthild of Magdeburg (p. 50)

For Mechthild, the heart of the gospel was the wedding of the human and the divine in the womb of Mary. This mystery of Word made flesh was not a litmus test of faith, but an entry point into contemplating the magnitude of the love of God. The incarnation is witness to an amazing love that so desires communion with humanity that anything is possible, even the birth of the Son of God. The virginity of Mary is testimony to the trust and faithfulness that bring forth new life. In this marriage of love and faith the Son of God is born. Mechthild is both awed by the completeness of Mary's devotion and inspired by her example to reach new heights of faith in the power of God's love.

The idea of the virgin birth strikes terror in the hearts of some Christians and defensive devotion in others. Yet every Advent all Christians read the first chapter of the gospel of Luke and wonder over the possibility that nothing is impossible with God. It is tempting to explain away this mystery or discard it as ancient history. It is possible to romanticize the naiveté of a young woman's faith. It is possible to sanitize and spiritualize the risk involved in her willingness to be the servant of God. As we distance ourselves from the impossible, we limit the possibility of God's entering our lives. We are challenged to stand, like Mary, in fear, in wonder, and in faith to see what is possible through the power of God.

Communion Meditation

In the beginning was the Word; and in the beginning was the Virgin who received that Word in flesh. Nothing in life requires more faith than the decision to bring new life into the world. We hear each day of scientific marvels that increase the possibilities of conception and of couples who rejoice over the miracle of birth. But nothing in our age matches the marvel of Mary's faith in the possibility of birth and her trust in the power of God to bring forth new life.

74

Miracles are not magic that defy explanation; they are simple acts of faith in God. Each week, we come to a table built on the faith of ordinary people who believed that nothing was impossible with God. With God, a young woman becomes the servant of salvation. With God, a carpenter is the Son of God. With God, a Savior rises from the ashes of death. With God, all things are possible.

Communion Prayer

God of grace and glory, we stand in awe before the mystery of salvation that comes to us in the marriage of divine desire and human faith. We marvel at the trust of a young woman who responded to your invitation to bear new life. At this table we lay before you the doubts that cloud our faith and pray for the voice of Gabriel to calm our fears. In this bread and this cup we bear witness to your power over life and death. As we partake of these elements, we witness to the possibilities of new life that are set before us this day. Here we stand; give us the courage to be your servants. For it is in the power of the One who dwells in us that we pray. Amen.

Suggestions for Celebration

Preparation: Have members of the congregation act out Luke 1:26–38. Follow the reading with a female vocalist singing "Her Baby, Newly Breathing" (*Chalice Hymnal,* #158).

Celebration: Read the communion meditation and prayer. During communion, play "Let All Mortal Flesh Keep Silence" (*Chalice Hymnal,* #124). After communion, sing the hymn together.

Standing with Mary in Humility

"For her humility was so great that she summoned the King to come to her. She was the strongest, that is undeniable."

Hadewijch of Brabant (p. 320)

Throughout history, Mary has been pictured as the humble servant who receives the Spirit of God. As a model of Christian womanhood, she exemplifies passivity, receptivity, powerlessness, and humble grace. But Hadewijch gives us a new understanding of humility. In her poems, she writes of humility as Mary's power. In humility Mary is able to embody the love of God as no king or prophet had done. Mary possesses a noble strength that tames God. Humility is not the opposite of pride, but the work of a confident self-assurance that receives the power of love with an open heart. Hadewijch teaches the young women under her care to open their hearts wide and deep and in so doing to find a strength that can conquer the world.

The image of Mary has been used for too long to reinforce the idea that a good Christian is selfless, passive, and powerless. But a close look at the gospel story shows us that Mary is anything but meek and mild. Hadewijch's description of humility reminds us that Christianity challenges our worldview and redefines the meaning of power. The power of our world is a power that controls, dominates, and divides. But the power of humility is a power that invites, includes, and unites. The power to tame God is the power to embody self-giving love. Nothing is lowlier, and nothing transforms the world more.

Communion Meditation

Mary's song, found in Luke 1:46–55, is one of the most ironic passages in all of scripture. Here a young woman speaks of the ability of God to transform the powers of the world. The mighty are brought down, and the lowly are lifted up. There is strength in God's mercy and justice for the humble. Salvation is not success; it is faithfulness to the covenant of God. In a mild voice, Mary challenges us all to contemplate what it means to find favor with God.

Two thousand years after her magnificent song, we still struggle to catch a vision of God's realm. The church has grown rich and powerful. We who live in the most prosperous nation in the course of history are tempted to assume we live in the city of God. But Mary's vision is one of a world transformed by the salvation of God. It is not merely a transformation of the powerful and the powerless; it is a transformation of the meaning of power. Here at this table we continue to sing her song as we share the bread of salvation and drink the cup of blessing. As we do so, we receive the power of God poured out for the redemption of the world.

Communion Prayers

Before Communion: Mighty One, we bow before your throne this day. Here on this table we see Christ's body lifted up for the nourishment of the world and Christ's blood poured out to quench the thirst of the world. We sing with Mary of the magnitude of your favor and proclaim to the world the salvation offered by your grace.

Our souls magnify you, O Lord, and our spirits rejoice in God our Savior. Amen.

After Communion: Mighty One, we rise from this table with our hunger for righteousness satisfied and our thirst for justice quenched. Pour out upon us the strength of your humble love, and fill us with the power of your grace. In the name of the risen Christ we go forth to lift up the lowly and fill the hungry with good things.

Our souls magnify you, O Lord, and our spirits rejoice in God our Savior. Amen.

Suggestions for Celebration

Preparation: Read and sing together the responsive reading "Song of Mary" (*Chalice Hymnal,* #131). Read the communion meditation and sing together "My Soul Gives Glory to My God" (*Chalice Hymnal,* #130).

Celebration: Read the prayer before communion. During the sharing of communion, sing "Give Thanks" (*Chalice Hymnal,* #528). After communion, read the closing prayer.

Standing with Mary in Justice

"This figure who is leaning against the pillars represents God's Justice . . . She is as white and translucent as an unruffled cloud."

Hildegard of Bingen (*Scivias,* p. 467)

Hildegard's visions are filled with female figures that symbolize the virtues of Christian life. Here Justice is shown as a huge female form that looks over the earth with the law of God. She reaches from heaven to earth in the incarnation and shines forth in the Son of God. Her flame burns on in the minds of those who obey the justice of God. Beside her stand Strength and Purity, which together with Justice work to bring forth the realm of God. All are represented as female forms because it is through Mary that the Word breathed out the whole of the virtues upon the earth. Likewise, it is through the daughters and sons of Mary that justice continues to be born throughout the earth.

All of Hildegard's writing was meant to inspire the nuns under her care to grow in virtue and to work for the coming of God's realm. She believed that salvation in Christ empowered Christians to work for justice, stand up against unrighteousness, and show mercy to the stranger. She knew that the church was called to bring justice to the world and, despite all evidence to the contrary, would live up to its calling. She inspired all she met to stay true to the strength of their convictions and to remain unstained by the corruption of the world. Inspired by the Holy Spirit, filled with the vision of Christ, surrounded by Mary and all the faithful through the ages, Hildegard worked for the justice of God.

Communion Meditation

At the communion table we witness the birth pangs of the justice of God. It was at the first communion table in the upper room that Jesus reminded his disciples to share bread and wine in his name. The first Christians understood this meal to be shared with all who gathered in his name regardless of background or status. They not only broke bread and shared wine; they also shared their wealth, and cared for the poor. In this way they prepared the way for the eschatological banquet that awaits us all in the realm of God.

What does it mean for you to share this bread today? With whom will you share the bread of life? Who is crying for the cup of blessing? As we eat this bread and drink this cup we are called to be the Body of Christ in the world. We remember that his body extends beyond this fellowship to the ends of the earth. Whenever we feed the hungry, clothe the naked, or visit the sick, we commune with Christ. For when we minister unto the least of them, we minister unto him who calls us together in his name.

Communion Prayer

Flame of Justice, we gather at this table of blessing to partake in the banquet of salvation. Here we bear witness to the bounty of creation that is entrusted to our care for the nourishment of the world. We stand in the presence of your righteousness poured out in mercy for all. Give us the courage to shine forth with your justice, as our ancestors did long ago. For here we give praise to the One who sits in glory for the judgment of the world. Amen.

Suggestions for Celebration

Preparation: Read Matthew 25:31–46 and Acts 2:43–47. Sing together verses one through three of "Restless Weaver" (*Chalice Hymnal* #658).

Celebration: Read together the communion meditation and prayer. After communion, sing together verse four of the hymn.

Standing with Mary in Reason

"I saw in the spirit a queen come in, clad in a gold dress; and her dress was all full of eyes...And I said: Yes indeed! Long enough have you caused me woe and pain! You are my soul's faculty of Reason."

Hadewijch of Brabant (p. 285)

For Hadewijch, reason is the queen of the virtues. Reason is the ability to see things truthfully, especially the truth of one's ability to love. It is reason that haunts Hadewijch with the knowledge that no one can perfectly love God. While Hadewijch is tempted to linger in the spiritual highs of her religious life, reason brings her back to earth and reminds her that she has a responsibility to share God's love with others in acts of service. Reason keeps Hadewijch striving in love, searching for truth, and growing in faith. Hadewijch writes that even Mary, full of silent reasoning and humble love, does not fully see God until her assumption into heaven. We stand with Mary clothed in reason and looking forward to the fullness of God.

This vision was an important reminder to Hadewijch that reason is not opposed to faith, but clarifies and strengthens it. Reason is the search for truth; and all truth, whether it is truth about the nature of the universe, the dynamics of the human psyche, or the foundations of our faith, can increase our love for God. By claiming her power of reason, Hadewijch was able to use her mind, as well as her heart, to glorify God. Reason, she writes, taught her to live the truth. May we too use all our faculties to know and serve God.

Communion Meditation

In his description of love the apostle Paul concludes his remarks by saying that now we see in a mirror dimly, but then we will see face-to-face. At this table, we catch a glimpse of the truth of God's saving love. In the face of Jesus we see the truth of God's mercy. In the words of invitation we see the body and blood that mirror the truth of God's sustaining presence and transforming power. In the community that gathers around this table we see dimly the truth of God's realm of justice and peace.

As we gather at this table we pray to be filled with silent reason and humble love. We seek clarity about the decisions that face us in this week. We long for a vision of God's realm that will lead us forward in the days ahead. We pray for wisdom to know the truth and to live it all our days. As we eat of this bread, symbol of the One who leads us in the way of truth and life, let us open our minds to the guiding reason of the Holy Spirit and pray for the courage to one day meet love face-to-face.

Communion Prayers

For the Bread: Holy Spirit, we come this day seeking a glimpse of your redeeming love. At this table we hear the truth of righteousness, we see the path of salvation, we taste the bread of heaven. Shine on us this day with the wisdom of the ages and join us in the fellowship of kindred minds. Bound together in the truth of Christian love, we pray. Amen.

For the Cup: Guiding light, we stand in the beam of your shining grace. At this table we bear witness to your steadfast love, we stand in the shadow of the glory of the cross, we drink the cup of eternal blessing. Break through the shadows that cloud our vision, and open before us the path of salvation. In the name of the Sun of salvation we pray. Amen.

Suggestions for Celebration

Preparation: Read Hadewijch's vision of reason found on pages 285–86 of her writings. Meditate on your own vision of reason and write down your description. Read 1 Corinthians 13:9–12.

Celebration: Sing together verses one, three, and five of "O God of Vision" (*Chalice Hymnal*, #288). Read the communion meditation and prayer. After communion, sing together "Blest Be the Tie That Binds" (*Chalice Hymnal*, #433).

Standing with Mary as Mother Church

*"May she, O Son, be your Bride for the restoration of My people;
may she be a mother to them, regenerating souls through the salvation of the Spirit and water."*

Hildegard of Bingen (*Scivias,* p. 237)

Featured prominently in Hildegard's picture of communion is a
woman dressed in bridal clothes with a crown on her head. She
stands beside the crucified Christ and is sprinkled by the blood and
water that pour from his side. She also kneels beside the communion
table and watches the mystery of bread and cup become the body
and blood of Christ as scenes from the incarnation and life of Christ
appear before her eyes. To the untrained eye, the woman might be
mistaken for the Virgin Mary standing at the side of her suffering
Son. The resemblance is striking and intentional. Hildegard writes
that as the Word became flesh in the womb of Mary to bring us
salvation, so the flesh, born in the womb of the church, regenerates
and restores life to the faithful. In communion we are reborn.

We may not share Hildegard's understanding of the
transformation of bread and wine, but we can learn from her that
communion is a vehicle by which we are given new life in Christ.
In communion the church enacts the story of salvation and we
participate in the mystery of the incarnation. Each time we share in
communion we are offered the sustenance of living water. It also
reminds us that the Body of Christ is a social reality. This connection
to the spirit of Christ does not happen in isolation but in the
community of faith. We are called to gather together around the
table to bear witness to the sacrament of salvation. Finally, Hildegard
reminds us that the work of the church is the work of nurture and
education. She calls communion the childbearing work of the church.
Around the table we witness the birth pangs of salvation and dedicate
ourselves to being the Body of Christ for the world.

Communion Meditation

Christ's promise to the church is that where two or three are
gathered in his name, he is there among them. Each week we gather

around the communion table as the church of Christ bearing witness to the promise that Christ dwells in our midst. As we break bread together we remember the Word made flesh in the womb of Mary and bear witness to the rebirth that we receive in the Body of Christ. In the cup that we drink we remember the blood of salvation poured out for the redemption of the world, and we drink the living water that restores our souls. Here we receive the power to bind injustice and to break loose the captive. Come partake in the living Body of our Savior, Christ the Lord.

Communion Prayers

Before Communion: Holy, holy, holy Lord, God of power and might. Heaven and earth are full of your glory, and holy is your name. We gather together with the church through the ages to give thanks for the mighty act of salvation that is born in our midst through the Word made flesh in the body of Jesus Christ. We are joined as one body in your name, and we gather around this one table to partake of the food of our salvation. As we raise this bread, symbol of the Body of Christ, we are bound together in one fellowship of love. As we pour this drink, symbol of the life-giving power of the blood of Christ, we are commissioned as your disciples to serve the world. Fill us with your Spirit so that we might be made holy and acceptable in your sight and become sacraments of your grace. Amen.

After Communion: Read the prayer "That the Church May Be One" (*Chalice Hymnal,* #394).

Suggestions for Celebration

Preparation: Read Matthew 18:20. Sing "Draw Us in the Spirit's Tether" (*Chalice Hymnal,* #392).

Celebration: Read the communion meditation and prayer. Pass the bread and cup around the table, serving one another the elements of communion. After communion, read together the concluding prayer.

Standing with Mary as Mother Earth

*"Your womb contained joy just as the grass was infused with Green-
ness, when the dew sank into it; Therefore Mother everything joyful has been created through you."*

Hildegard of Bingen (in Petroff, p.158)

Today Hildegard is best known for her musical compositions.
Many of her songs are written in praise of Mary as the mother of
salvation, and are filled with references to the goodness of the earth.
Mary is like a radiant white lily; her fertility is likened to a green
field; and the church praises her name with the break of a new dawn
on the horizon. All around her, Hildegard sees the beauty of creation,
and it reminds her of the creative work of God that bears fruit in the
womb of Mary. In Mary heaven and earth are joined in beautiful
harmony, and we are created to join in the song of creation.

A thousand years ago it was common to think of Mary as the
Mother of God. It is not so common today. But Hildegard's songs
have struck a chord with our concern for the earth. Her use of
nature images reminds us that salvation is the reconciliation of the
entire cosmos in the womb of God. We know that religions
throughout the ages have connected the fertility of the earth with
feminine forms of God. Christians throughout the ages have
understood Mary to represent the fertility of God. We can join with
them in praise of the beauty of the Earth and thanksgiving for the
ongoing work of our Creator.

Communion Meditation

Communion is a joyous celebration of the beauty of life. Here
at this table we place bread made from the grain of the fields, the
waters of the stream, and the salt of the earth. In the kneading of the
dough, we bear witness to the amazing creativity of God. The wine
that is shared at this table is filled with the fruit of the vine. In the
drinking of this cup we give thanks for the sweet taste of fertile soil
and the warm rays of the sun.

This bread and wine is the body and blood of our Savior come
to earth in the womb of Mary for the salvation of the world. As a

rose that blooms in radiant splendor, Christ comes into our midst full of the beauty of God. The One who cares for the lilies of the fields and the birds of the air shines upon us as the Sun of glory. Let us join with all the Earth in praise for the new dawn of creation.

Communion Prayer

Creator of us all, everywhere we look we see the majesty of your handiwork. In the smiling faces of children we see the hope you bring into the world. In the harmony of land and sky we see the peace that passes all understanding. In the flowers of the field we see the beauty of creation. And in the tender mercy of all your creatures we see your loving embrace.

Here at this table we see again the mystery of salvation. As bread is joined with wine we remember the harmony of heaven and earth that is joined in the womb of Mary. With Mary we behold the coming of your Spirit into our midst. May your creative spirit spring forth from us as it did from her, and may we join with Mary in praise to the glory of your creation. In our Savior's name we pray. Amen.

Suggestions for Celebration

Preparation: Set on the communion table a tree or branch to represent the family tree that joins us to Mary and all Christians throughout the ages. Read Luke 1:42. For a hymn of preparation, sing "Lo, How a Rose E'er Blooming" (*Chalice Hymnal,* #160).

Celebration: Read the communion prayer and meditation. During communion, listen to excerpts of Hildegard's music. One popular recording is entitled "Vision: The music of Hildegard von Bingen" (Angel Records, 1995). Other options include "Songs of Mary," written by John Bell (GIA publications, 1997) or "Womb of Life, and Source of Being" (*Chalice Hymnal,* #14).

CHAPTER 5

*Growing
Our Souls*

Growing Our Souls

"We become, in this way, gardens in bloom which the Lord beholds with pleasure so long as we continue to act in accord with the soul's plumbline."

Hildegard of Bingen (*Book of Divine Works*, p. 117)

Medieval women mystics are fascinating to us not only because of the richness of their descriptions of communion with God but also because of their desire to respond to this grace in the fullness of faith. Hildegard describes this response as growing our souls to become gardens that bloom in God's love. She writes about the earth as a metaphor for our lives. Our flesh is like the earth, our bones the rocks, our marrow the trees, and our souls the firmament that undergirds and directs our lives. The point of all this imagery is to remind us that we are creatures of God, and like all of creation, are made in order to be fruitful. To grow to our full potential requires a harmony of body and soul grounded in the soil of communion and nurtured by God's word.

Hildegard's own life is an inspiring example of growth. Her writing includes books on music, science, medicine, theology, and spiritual direction. She was also the administrator of two convents and a well-known preacher. At the age of sixty she began a preaching tour that urged her fellow Christians to use their talents for God's glory and the spreading of God's realm. A thousand years after her death, Christians are still challenged by her example to bloom in the fullness of God's grace.

Communion Meditation

In the parable of the sower, Jesus compares the life of faith to seeds that are planted on good soil and grow to bear fruit. The faithful hear the word of God, understand it, and live it out in lives of abundant grace. The musical *Godspell's* modern retelling of this parable in the song "All Good Gifts" reminds us that "we plow the fields and scatter the good seed on the land, but it is fed and watered by God's almighty hand."

Communion is the food and water given to us by God's own hand. It is a good gift given for the benefit of our souls and our growth in goodness and grace. As we come to communion this day let us reflect on the gifts that are bestowed on us. Where have we found morsels of bread that have filled our souls? Who has poured on us the cup of blessing? And what are we to do with these abundant gifts? Like seeds that are sown upon the earth, we can take root in the soil of God's grace. We can also be choked by weeds or eaten by birds of prey. Here at this table we find the rich soil that feeds our souls. Come receive the gifts of God.

Communion Prayer

Sun of heaven, we come to the communion table thankful for the abundant harvest set before us this day. All around us we see the goodness of your mercy in our lives. This community shines upon us with the warmth of Christian fellowship. This bread nurtures us with the presence of the living Word. This cup fills us with the blessing of redeeming grace. In our Savior Jesus Christ we see the green wheat of salvation rise from the dead soil of winter. May we bloom as the flowers of spring, bearing witness to the power of eternal life. In the name of our risen Savior we pray. Amen.

Suggestions for Celebration

Preparation: Read the parable of the sower found in Matthew 13:3–9, 18–23. Sing together "Now the Green Blade Rises" (*Chalice Hymnal,* #230).

Celebration: Read the communion meditation and prayer. During communion, play the song "All Good Gifts" from the musical *Godspell.* After communion, sing together the chorus of "All Good Gifts."

Growing Our Souls through Forgiveness

"Contrition seizes [us] by the inspiration of the Holy Spirit and turns bitterness into hope of God's mercy. And then the wounds begin to heal and the soul to revive."

Julian of Norwich (p. 244)

Julian lived during a time when growth in faith meant confession and absolution for sin. This process of contrition was developed to wear away sins through asking for forgiveness, receiving assurance of God's grace, and responding in acts of prayer and penitence. Julian's insight is that at the heart of this process is our need to forgive ourselves. We blame ourselves for our failings and shrink from God's grace by thinking we will sink into hell. But the act of contrition wears away this guilt through the hope of God's mercy, which washes over us on the wings of the Spirit. Growth requires forgiving ourselves, trusting in God, and waiting for our wounds to heal.

Julian does not reveal how this process worked in her own life. However, we read in Margery Kempe's autobiography that Julian gave Margery this very advice and urged her to persevere in faith. There is a little bit of Margery in each of us. We all are tempted to despair in our unworthiness. But Julian reminds us that people who cling to such feelings actually dishonor God because they fail to trust in the power of the Spirit that turns bitterness into hope and to participate in the rituals of the church that offer healing and wholeness. Our growth begins with the revival of our faith in God.

Communion Meditation

Forgiveness is so difficult. As we come to the communion table we remember Jesus' plea for forgiveness and yet we wonder how he could think of forgiving those who crucified him. Maybe that is why he cries out to God in anguish, hoping that his Father can provide the forgiveness that he himself cannot give from the cross. Earlier he had taught his disciples that forgiveness is received as it is granted. "Forgive," he said, "and you will be forgiven."

What prayer for forgiveness do you bring to the communion table this day? If it is a prayer to be forgiven, then come to receive the cup of blessing. If it is a prayer to forgive, then come to share in the bread of heaven. We share in a Lord who promises to give rest to all who are weary and heavy laden. Forgiveness shines down from the cross as a beacon that brightens the dark recesses of our souls. Come share the Lord who enters our lives for the forgiveness of sins.

Communion Prayers

Before Communion: God of grace and glory, we come to this table eager to share in the body and blood of our Lord Jesus Christ. At this table, we long for the forgiveness that is offered in this meal for the healing of our souls. We confess the sins that keep us from growing in faith and pray that this bread will fill us with the sweet taste of your mercy. We place before you the bitterness that festers in our hearts and hope that this cup of forgiveness will empower us to forgive others. Come into our presence this day as we pray together the prayer given to us by our Savior. *(Pray the Lord's Prayer.)*

After Communion: God of grace and glory, in this communion hour we have tasted a measure of your abiding grace. In the distance we hear the hosannas of angels and see the glory of your realm. Lead us on to the feast of blessing that awaits us in our eternal home. In our Lord's name we pray. Amen.

Suggestions for Celebration

Preparation: Read Luke 6:37–38. Read the communion meditation. Read together the communion prayer followed by the Lord's Prayer. After the prayer, have people stand for an assurance of pardon. "In Jesus Christ you are forgiven. Come, take the bread; come, drink the wine; come, share the Lord." Then sing together "Come, Share the Lord" (*Chalice Hymnal,* #408).

Celebration: Share in communion. Afterward, read together the closing prayer.

Growing our Souls through Relationships

"That is how I show you that you are my true daughter, yes and mother also, and sister, wife and spouse."

Margery Kempe (p. 57)

For Margery, growth meant learning how to balance the many relationships in her family. She was the daughter of the local mayor, married to a local businessman at the age of twenty, and mother to fourteen children. She also longed to be a devout Christian, good sister to her neighbors, and follower of Christ. For a long time, Margery thought the only way to be a Christian was to give up her family relationships. But then she remembered the scripture that declares that whoever does the will of God is Jesus' brother, sister, and mother. Margery began to understand that she could be a daughter in her devotion, mother in her mourning, sister in her compassion, and wife in her longing for God.

There is a modern appeal to Margery's quest. Christians today juggle a multitude of roles in their family, work, and church lives. We can feel ourselves pulled between competing commitments for our time and affection. Often the church adds to this stress by making members feel guilty for their lack of devotion to its programs and services. To grow in faith requires a fresh perspective. Is it possible that people such as Margery show us that we are not asked to choose between our commitments, but to learn to balance them instead? Do we need to learn that God is not on the edges of our lives, but at the center, filling us with grace to be in full relationship with self, God, and world? Balance comes from discerning the connections between all that we are and all that we have been given in relation to God.

Communion Meditation

We often call our community the family of God. Here we are sisters and brothers in Christ. We remember Jesus' words that whoever does the will of God is his brother, sister, and mother. This idea of the church as a family is both a bane and a blessing. Here we can find a new community of belonging that offers to us the love and acceptance of being at home in God. But here we can also find the worst of family relationships. The table can be surrounded by sibling rivalries, parent-child conflicts, and abusive spousal relationships.

Jesus offers a fresh perspective on family life. We gather around the table with all our family histories and are called to join together in one family of faith. We lift up the beauty of divine love and brotherly compassion found in Christ. We are offered the opportunity to grow in our devotion, witness, and longing for God. At this table we are brothers, sisters, mothers, fathers, and followers of our Lord Jesus Christ.

Communion Prayer

Heavenly Father, merciful Mother, holy Brother, almighty God, we gather at this table as one family joined together by your grace. We bring to you all the relationships of our lives, grateful for the many blessings bestowed upon each of us, and asking for your guidance to love and cherish all who are in our care. At this table we gather with your church around the world. Help us to extend the fellowship of this table to all whom we meet. As this bread nourishes us, remind us of our duty to feed the world. As this cup refreshes us, remind us of our calling to carry your blessing to all whom we meet. For in you we are brothers and sisters, one in Christ. Amen.

Suggestions for Celebration

Preparation: Read Mark 3:31–35. Explain that this is the scripture that helped Margery Kempe grow in her faith. Discuss together what this scripture means to each person gathered for communion. Sing together "Who Is My Mother, Who Is My Brother?" (*Chalice Hymnal,* #486).

Celebration: Read the communion meditation and prayer. After communion, read a prayer for families found on pages 169–71 of *Chalice Worship.*

Growing Our Souls through Knowledge

"Speak therefore of these wonders, and, being so taught, write them and speak."

Hildegard of Bingen (*Scivias*, p. 59)

The title *Scivias* is shorthand for "Know the Ways of the Lord." The work begins with a moving account of Hildegard's own calling to write theology. At the age of forty-two she hears a voice commanding her to speak and write. She confesses that she has received tremendous insights since she was a child, actually seeing pictures of the cosmos that explain the mysteries of God. But she is afraid to share her ideas. In her day, women were not allowed to teach, not even Benedictine nuns, who were among the most learned people of their day. Now having been told to speak, she begins a writing career that will encourage countless Christians to grow in their knowledge of God.

One of the greatest desires among people in the pew is knowledge of their faith. Bookstores are filled with books on spirituality that open up the world of the greatest thinkers through the ages. The growing small-group movement in local churches provides an opportunity for laity to be part of a learning community. Those who are fortunate to study at a seminary are amazed at the vast resources of biblical studies, theology, and history. They feel like Alice in Wonderland, entering a world turned upside down, but filled with insight and new adventure. In all these ways, we are given the opportunity to follow in Hildegard's footsteps and know the ways of God.

Communion Meditation

What does it mean to come to communion with our whole being, our mind as well as our soul? We are commanded to love God with our heart, soul, mind, and strength, and yet we are tempted to think that we have to believe in a salvation we cannot understand. The saving grace offered to us in Christ is truly a mystery, but it is not unknowable. As we strive to understand the meaning of the incarnation, to study the teaching of Jesus, and to contemplate the relevance of the cross, we are led to deeper and deeper resources of faith. And we rejoice in the ability to use our God-given intelligence to glorify our Creator.

At this table we gather with the sages of all times. Here we eat with Paul, who first taught the gospel to the Gentiles. At our side we see Hildegard, whose illuminations have opened the eyes of many to the knowledge of God. Close by are the Sunday school teachers and pastors who have inspired our journeys in faith. Spread before us is the book of life. Let us gather together at the table of the great Teacher, who showed us all the way to God.

Communion Prayer

Holy Wisdom, everywhere we turn we see the majesty of your creation. In the stars that brighten the dark night we learn the vastness of your universe. In the study of the smallest of your creatures, we see the complexity of your world. From all that surrounds us we learn of the rhythm that pulses throughout your creation. Artists try to portray your beauty; poets write praises to your name; musicians play sweet strains in harmony for your glory.

But only here at this table do we understand the mystery of your grace. Here we hear the words of salvation taught by your Son. Here we taste the bread of heaven that fills us with knowledge. Here we share the cup of blessing that feeds our minds. Here we come to grow in strength and knowledge of you. Illumine us we pray. Amen.

Suggestions for Celebration

Preparation: Read Mark 12:30. Discuss together the teachers that have meant the most to you. Sing together "Sing of a God in Majestic Divinity" (*Chalice Hymnal*, #331).

Celebration: Read the communion meditation and prayer. After the sharing of communion, sing "Open My Eyes, That I May See" (*Chalice Hymnal*, #586).

Growing Our Souls through Virtue

"I find all satisfaction in virtues and faithfully climb from virtue to virtue."

Hildegard of Bingen (*Book of Divine Works,* p. 39)

Knowledge of God led Hildegard to strive to do God's will. Over and over again in her writing she stresses that the Christian life is a life of virtue and good works. It is based in the virtues of faith, hope, and love, and lives out these virtues in works for justice. And it is possible to be faithful because our lives are infused with the grace of God. She pictures the life of faith as bridged by a ladder of virtues that descends from Christ to the heart of the faithful and ascends up to God in good works. In this way Christians are given the task of building up the Body of Christ. Virtue truly is its own reward, for when we do good works, Hildegard says, we touch God.

A few years ago a book recommended doing random acts of kindness. Examples included paying the toll for the car behind you on the highway or leaving an anonymous note of thanks on a coworker's desk. The point was that such acts make you feel good and give you the satisfaction that you have helped to make the world a better place. Hildegard reminds us that God has decreed a plan for making the world a better place, and it is embodied in the life of Jesus Christ. As we follow his example and are guided by his teachings, we participate in building up the realm of God. Such work brings purpose to our lives and gives us hope for the future. Virtue is its own reward.

Communion Meditation

When is the last time you read the Sermon on the Mount? Jesus teaches the crowd that in him the law has been fulfilled. Those who hunger and thirst for righteousness will be filled; those who work for peace will be called the children of God. The life of faith offered to us in Jesus Christ is not an easy life or a self-centered life; rather, it is a life of good works that shine before others and give glory to God. Through Christ we are given the grace to heal relationships, to be faithful, to keep true to our word, and to practice love.

These are words that have challenged and confounded Christians for all time. Is it really possible to turn the other cheek? Can one really overcome temptation to sin? At this table we celebrate the perfection of humanity in Jesus Christ and the spiritual food that makes us part of the Body of Christ. We receive the bread of life so that we will no longer hunger for meaning or direction. We receive the wine of salvation so that we will no longer thirst with temptation or harmful desire. We remember the words of our Savior to be perfect even as the One in whose image we are made is the perfection of the universe. Come to the table to receive the blessings of God.

Communion Prayer

Word of God, we stand at your table of righteousness to satisfy our hunger and quench our thirst. Here we remember the words of blessing that have guided your people through the ages. In this tasty bread we remember that you have called us to be the salt of the earth. In this shining cup we hear the call to become the light of the world. We come to this table remembering the One who is the pioneer and perfecter of our faith, and join ourselves with him in one body. We long to follow in the path of blessedness. Guide us we pray. Amen.

Suggestions for Celebration

Preparation: Read Matthew 5. Read and sing together "The Beatitudes" (*Chalice Hymnal*, #185).

Celebration: Read the communion meditation and prayer. After sharing in communion, sing together "I Would Be True" (*Chalice Hymnal*, #608).

Growing Our Souls through Service

"The only rest of such a heart is to do its utmost for the sake of its Beloved ...and to offer him noble service as a gift."

Hadewijch of Brabant (p. 71)

Hadewijch lived during a time when knights served their lords in noble service. Knights took vows of loyalty to serve their lords to the death, and for their service they received protection and support. It was an honorable and well-ordered life. Hadewijch urged her readers to be noble servants of God. In doing so, she gave the women under her care the courage to risk all for the sake of God. She advised them to serve others in all ways, but to remember their noble birth. Beguines were not asked to lose themselves; rather, they were to find their identity in serving God. Hadewijch herself confessed that serving God is true satisfaction.

Today we do not think of service in terms of chivalry and noble love. But we still speak of serving God, and we still try to understand what it means to do God's will. Hadewijch reminds us that we are created for a purpose, and that purpose brings dignity to our lives. She also reminds us that service should never be confused with servitude. She was not a servile woman, and she advised those under her care to stand up and fight for justice. However, she did not confuse service with success. We are to be compassionate towards others, but ultimately it is God who protects, guides, and brings the world to its fruition. Our job is to do all we can to be a part of that grand plan. Doing so is the way to live up to our calling as servants of God.

Communion Meditation

At any table there is a seating order. The host sits at the head, and honored guests sit nearby. So it is not surprising that the disciples wanted to know the pecking order of their own fellowship. But Jesus chastises them for their quest for greatness and teaches them that God's order is not based on power and privilege, but on service and care for the children of God. It is a table that is spread by the grace of God, and all, even Jesus himself, find their place around the table of God.

The table of Christian fellowship is spread with hospitality for all. It is not based on who you are or what riches you can bring to the meal. The only requirement of this table is that you come and take your place as part of the Body of Christ. To eat of this bread and drink of this cup is to recognize your calling as a servant of God. To take part in this meal is an acknowledgment of your desire to follow in the footsteps of the One who dedicated his life to the service of God. Here we find our common calling to serve each child as a child of God.

Communion Prayer

Lord of lords, around this table we gather with those in the upper room to follow in the service of our Savior, Christ the Lord. You have made the heavens and the earth, and all creation bows before your throne. At this table we feast on bread and wine, mindful of the banquet that you have set for us in all eternity. As we raise our cups in praise we dedicate ourselves in noble service to your realm. In Jesus' name we pray. Amen.

Suggestions for Celebration

Preparation: Read Mark 9:33–37. Gather everyone around the communion table, including the children. Read the communion meditation and prayer. Sing together "Lead On, O King Eternal" (*Chalice Hymnal* #632).

Celebration: If it is not your practice to serve children communion, consider a way to include them in your meal. Have them receive a blessing at the communion table, or a snack of goldfish crackers and juice. After communion, sing together "I Bind My Heart This Tide" (*Chalice Hymnal,* #350).

Growing Our Souls through Struggle

"We must continually dare to fight her in new assaults with all our strength, all our knowledge, all our wealth, all our love—all these alike. This is how to behave with the Beloved."

Hadewijch of Brabant (p. 64)

Hadewijch must have been a feisty woman. She identifies herself with Jacob as one who wrestles with God. This struggle is not a fight against God, but an attempt to catch hold of all of God's love. Just as Jacob would not let go until he received a blessing, so she keeps striving to receive the blessing of God's love. This ability to struggle and strive for more from our relationship with God is an expression of our innate freedom. The person who has never fought with God, she writes, has never lived a free day. We are free to be in relationship with the source of all love. Such freedom requires devoting all that we are—our strength, knowledge, wealth, and love—to be with God.

Hadewijch challenges us to seek ways to grow in our faith. It seems a bit irreverent to think of ourselves as fighting God. Yet we do it every day. We fight against the idea of following God's will. We struggle with the idea of being called as servants of God. What would it mean to think of this wrestling of our souls as our attempt to grow in our faith? What would it mean to reach the depths of our longing and passion in our love for God? Dare to catch hold of God's love, Hadewijch says, before Love passes us by.

Communion Meditation

Do you ever wrestle with the idea of communion? Even Jesus struggled with drinking this cup. In the garden of Gethsemane he prayed for this cup to pass from him. He knew that the cup that we drink is a cup of pain and sorrow. He knew that the path before him was filled with disappointment and betrayal. He knew that being the Son of God was not a life of ease and comfort, but rather, offered him the challenge of being one with the entire world. And yet like Jacob he continued to wrestle until this cup became for him a cup of blessing.

What cup is prepared for you this day? At communion we are given the opportunity to reflect on our life of faith. If we dare, we can gaze on this table and see reflected here the will of God. We can receive from this table the strength to follow that will to the ends of the earth. As we journey along the way, we will walk alongside all those who have struggled to see God. Like Jacob we are able to hold on; like Hadewijch we are challenged to grow in the fullness of faith; like Jesus we are free to follow the will of God. Come and drink the cup of blessing.

Communion Prayers

For the Bread: O Lord, we gather at this table with the faithful through the ages. In their lives of faith we see the challenge of growing into the fullness of your love. As we eat this bread we are reminded of the Son of God, who taught us how to be faithful and true. May this bread of heaven fill us with the courage to do your will. Amen.

For the Cup: O Lord, in this cup we see the blessing that is promised for all those who struggle for righteousness. As fruit that ripens on the vine, we are called to ripen into the fullness of faith. Help us to overcome our fears and fill us with the courage to follow in your footsteps. May this cup be for us the cup of blessing. Amen.

Suggestions for Celebration

Preparation: Read Genesis 32:24–31 and Matthew 26:36–39. Discuss the struggles and blessings of your lives. Sing together verses one, two, and four of "I Am Thine, O Lord" (*Chalice Hymnal,* #601).

Celebration: Read the communion meditation and prayer. During communion, sing "We Are Climbing Jacob's Ladder." After communion, sing verse three of "I Am Thine, O Lord."

Growing Our Souls through Communion

"But now we are satisfied, for we drink in Him the saving cup, tasting Who God is in true faith."

Hildegard of Bingen (*Scivias*, p. 256)

Hildegard describes communion as the food of life and the true medicine of our souls. It is in the act of communion that one is refreshed in the Spirit, restored to life, and strengthened in faith. It is here that one can literally touch the source of salvation and take that saving grace into one's heart. It is here that we taste God. She writes that it is communion that makes one green and fruitful. It was for communion that she composed her beautiful music and during communion that she received her deepest insights. Gladdened by this sacrament, she writes, one may attain supernal strength.

We would do well to remember that communion is the source of our growth in faith. To grow in forgiveness, relationships, knowledge, virtue, service, or struggle requires superhuman strength. And this is exactly what is offered to us in the act of communion. Our strength comes from eating manna from heaven and tasting the possibility of new life. We hear again the story of our salvation and glimpse a foretaste of the redemption of the world. In communion, we commune with God.

Communion Meditation

Do you remember a time when you communed with God? Think about the way the bread tasted in your mouth and the feel of communion on your lips. Try to remember the sounds of the service and the voice of affirmation in your heart. Recall the comfort of belonging to the Body of Christ. Give thanks for the power to restore life and walk in faith.

Today and every day you are offered the opportunity to commune with God. Christians through the ages have approached this table eager to receive the bread of heaven. And they have been satisfied. Like them we come to this table longing for the touch of God and the taste of salvation. We are strengthened by the promise of Jesus that this bread is the bread of life. We surround ourselves with the witness of the faithful that in Christ we are offered the wellspring of everlasting life. May our memories fill us with the conviction that God is present in this meal, and our faith propel us to come in hope of being restored in the Body of Christ.

Communion Prayers

For the Bread: Spirit of the living God, we pray that in this communion hour you will fall upon our spirits and fill us with the power of new life. We see in this bread the Body of Christ come to earth to be for us the food of salvation. We long to follow in his path and be the Body of Christ in the world. Fill us with your presence in this communion hour. Bread of heaven, feed us in your grace. Amen.

For the Cup: Spirit of the living God, we stand before this cup of salvation mindful of the thirst that parches our souls. We fill our mouths with the sweet taste of the world, but still we are not satisfied. We long for the wellspring of living water that can wash the stains from our lives and restore us to your grace. Fill our cups, Lord, fill them up, and make us whole. Amen.

Suggestions for Celebration

Preparation: Read John 6:48–51. Read the communion meditation. Share together the most meaningful communion experiences of your lives. Sing together "Fill My Cup, Lord" (*Chalice Hymnal,* #351).

Celebration: Read the communion prayer. During communion, continue to play the same hymn. After communion, have a soloist sing "May the Blessing of God" (*Chalice Hymnal,* #448).

CHAPTER 6

*Sharing
Our Sorrows*

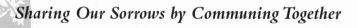

Sharing Our Sorrows by Communing Together

*"I could scarcely endure that anyone should love him less than I.
And charity for others wounded me cruelly."*

Hadewijch of Brabant (p. 292)

It may seem odd to begin a section on sharing with this quote from Hadewijch. She was a demanding person and had a hard time accepting others. She expected everyone to be as devout in faith as she was and to risk all for the sake of love. When they failed to meet her expectations, she was anguished by their disregard for God. When they excelled in faith, she was fearful that her own love was being diminished. She imagined herself as a young eagle flying with another through the realm of God. At first the vision disturbed her because she wanted to be alone in God. Then she realized that this was a lesson about the role of others in the love of God. She could love others in a proper way without being critical or jealous. With this insight she was able to commune with God.

We may be tempted to think of communion as a solitary moment. It is one of the few times when we can put aside the responsibilities and demands of daily life and rest in God. But communion is by definition a community event. We can pray by ourselves, but only in community can we celebrate the Body of Christ. The act of communion is a reminder that we live in community and that we share with one another the joys and sorrows of our lives. Like it or not, we fly with others toward the realm of God.

Communion Meditation

Being a community of faith is hard work. We live in a society that both realizes the interconnectedness of the world and preaches that we can make it on our own. In the midst of such mixed messages it is easy to grieve over the sorrows of others and agonize over the effect that others have on our lives.

Maybe you come to this table today grieving over the reluctance of a family member to accept the salvation offered in Christ. Or maybe your participation at this table is diminished by pettiness and disagreement in your community. We come to communion surrounded by all those in our community. At this table stand our enemies, our friends, our loved ones, and our neighbors. Some of these people encourage our love for God while others test it. Some live troubled lives that grieve our hearts. Others live exemplary lives that challenge our faith.

Maybe this is why the apostle Paul wrote that he wished he was cut off from Christ for the sake of his own people. He understood how hard it was for his people to accept the good news of salvation in Christ. And yet he realized that their hope was realized in this redemption. He knew that we come as one to commune in the Spirit of the Lord.

Communion Prayer

Holy Trinity, we come to this table united as one in your Spirit. You exist in perfect harmony. Help us to live in the harmony of your love. You sustain us in diversity. Guide us as we strive to respect the dignity of all. You redeem us in Christ. Help us to spread the good news of salvation. In the name of all those whom we love we pray. Amen.

Suggestions for Celebration

Preparation: Read Romans 9:3. In a time of prayer lift up the names of those people you long to meet at the communion table. End the time of prayer by reading Romans 9:15.

Celebration: Read the communion meditation and prayer. Sing together "They'll Know We Are Christians" (*Chalice Hymnal*, #494). During communion, sing or play (on the flute or other woodwind instrument) "Weave" (*Chalice Hymnal*, #495).

Sharing Our Sorrows by Being Connected in Christ

"No more apathy now, my sweetest children, because the blood has begun to flow and to receive life!"

Catherine of Siena
(in letters edited by Noffke, p. 111)

One of the most dramatic and bloodiest moments of Catherine's life was her witness of the execution of a young man in her hometown of Siena. Moments before his execution she visited him and shared communion with him. He felt strengthened by Catherine's presence and begged her to stay at his side. As his head was lowered to the block she reminded him of his destiny in everlasting life. With his last breath he cried out the names of Jesus and Catherine, while his severed head fell into her lap. At that moment, Catherine saw a vision of Jesus receiving the young man's blood into his side and his soul into his heart. Catherine remained on the platform clothed in blood and at peace in the knowledge of eternal life.

The image of this tiny woman covered in blood is a vivid symbol of the solidarity of the community in Christ. Her defiance of this act of injustice spoke louder than any words she could have preached against her community. But what is most touching about this event is her concern for the man's welfare. She visited him in prison because she wanted to console his troubled soul. She took him to worship because she wanted to strengthen his faith. She agreed to remain at his side because she wanted to stand in solidarity with him at his death. She did all this because she knew she was connected to this man in the blood of Christ. As she reminds her readers, there is no room for apathy in the Body of Christ. We are one blood.

Communion Meditation

The apostle Paul writes that the cup that we share is a participation in the blood of Christ. What does it mean to participate in the blood of Christ? Catherine of Siena understood blood as a symbol of the profound connectedness of the community of faith. Christ's blood is the sign of God's presence in our lives. Through his blood we see the participation of divine power in the course of human history. To share this cup is to commit ourselves to care for one another. As we do we bear witness to the injustice of innocent blood shed for the sins of the world, and we cast our gaze upon the redemption of that blood in the realm of God.

Communion Prayer

Living Bread of God, we come as seeds scattered in the field, fractured from one another by our individual needs and struggling to come into the light of your salvation. As we meet here at this table, knead us into one body worthy to share in the Body of Christ. Strengthen the ties that unite us to one another and to the coming of your realm. May this cup be for us a taste of your redemption, filling us with the power to participate in the outpouring of your blessing upon the Earth. In the unity of the Living Vine we pray. Amen.

Suggestions for Celebration

Preparation: Read 1 Corinthians 10:16–17. Tell Catherine's story and discuss together the meaning of participating in the blood of Christ. Sing together "Seed, Scattered and Sown" (*Chalice Hymnal*, #395).

Celebration: Read the communion meditation and prayer. Share in communion by breaking one loaf of bread and drinking from one cup of blessing. As you pass the bread, say, "Is this bread that we share not a participation in the Body of Christ?" As you pass the cup, say, "Is this cup not a participation in the blood of Christ?" After communion, sing together the chorus of the communion hymn.

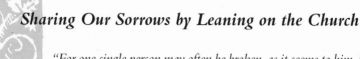

Sharing Our Sorrows by Leaning on the Church

"For one single person may often be broken, as it seems to him, but the entire body of Holy Church was never broken, nor ever will be without end."

Julian of Norwich (p. 301)

Julian knew that sharing our sorrows means not only caring for others but also receiving from them the comfort of Christ. She urges her readers to lean on the church because it is here that one receives the mercy of Christ and the protection of the community of faith. Hers is a vision of the power of the community to keep hope and faith alive. Its message has a timeless quality that puts daily struggles in perspective. Its strong walls and solid foundation offer protection. Maybe this is why she chose to live in a room attached to a church in Norwich, England. Her strength came from being able to literally lean on the community of faith.

We know that the church is a sanctuary with a long history of protecting the weak and offering hospitality to the stranger. It is also a refuge for our souls. In communion, we share our sorrows with the community of faith. Here we confess our sins and are washed clean. Here we expose our wounds and receive healing care. Here we release our fears and are held in safety. To be part of the Body of Christ is an invitation to rest in the arms of the community of faith. What do you need to share with the Body of Christ this day?

Communion Meditation

We come to worship adorned with smiles that mask the reality of our lives. Why do we hide our sorrows? Is this not the place where we remember the One who suffered and died for the sins of the world? Is this not the table where we eat broken bread? At this table we witness the miracle of the renewal of life and the unity of the Body of Christ. This is a sanctuary that is strong enough to carry the sorrows of our lives and caring enough to offer protection from all harm.

The book of James gives us a beautiful picture of the church as a sharing community. He writes that in suffering, ask for the prayers of the church. In joy, raise your voice in praise. In sickness, be anointed with healing oil. In wrongdoing, confess your sins and receive forgiveness. In all things and at all times, we are called to share our lives in the Body of Christ. Come to communion and lean on the loving arms of the church.

Communion Prayer

Almighty God, Creator of the universe and Redeemer of our lives, we come to you this day joined as one in the Body of Christ. We bear witness to the mighty act of salvation that formed the earth and filled it with light. We remember your people Israel, who were guided through the wilderness by the flame of your Spirit. We give thanks for your Son and our Savior, who taught us your truth and opened for us the gate of salvation.

As we eat this bread and drink from this cup we remember that the salvation of the world is offered to us this day. As we eat this bread we place our lives in your hands and ask for your healing touch to mend our hearts and heal our wounds. As we drink from this cup we lean on the power of your presence to hear our sorrows, and ask for your comfort to wash away our cares. As this meal strengthens our bodies, so we give thanks for this community that satisfies our souls. For it is in the love of the Body of Christ that we pray. Amen.

Suggestions for Celebration

Preparation: Read together James 5:13–16. Have a time for sharing and prayer. Sing together verses one through three of "Sister, Let Me Be Your Servant" (*Chalice Hymnal,* #490).

Celebration: Read the communion meditation and prayer. After communion, sing verses four and five of the hymn.

Sharing Our Sorrows by Crying for Christ

"Sir, his dying is as present to me now as if it were this very morning that he died. And I think it should feel the same to you, and to anyone who calls himself a Christian."

Margery Kempe (p. 211)

Margery could hardly look at a picture of Christ crucified without breaking into tears. She wept for the kindness extended to her in Christ and the pain of his death. This overt display of compassion elicited a variety of reactions. A priest seeing her weep told her to gain her composure. After all, he said, Jesus had been dead for a long time. She snapped back with this retort about the present reality of Christ's death and suggested that it was his piety, not hers, that was in question. A friend commented that Margery was a good example of faith and witness to a grace-filled soul.

We come to communion longing to feel the presence of the living God. It is a presence that comes to us in the stark reality of existence. As we look at the communion table we see the pain of the cross and hear the anguish of his labored breath. We smell the vinegar on his lips and the blood dripping from his side. The test of faith is how we react to this scene. When we hide our faces or explain away his pain, we harden our hearts to the reality of God. When we face the cross and dare to share in its sorrow, our hearts are warmed by the wonders of divine grace, our eyes are opened to injustice, and compassion fills our souls. It is a strange form of blessing, but our comfort comes from nothing less than mourning for the Son of God.

Communion Meditation

We know little of the reality of suffering. Hospitals sanitize the smell of the dying, and modern medicine eases the pain. Many have never seen a person die and have a hard time feeling the agony and sorrow depicted in the daily news. When tragedy does strike our lives, we are tempted to deny it or move away from its sting. We give ourselves little time for grieving and little space for sharing in the sorrow of the world.

112

But here at this table we see a man suffering in agony. His innocent death is an outrage to our sense of justice. His pain is an assault on our sense of decency and order. His suffering is a challenge to our desire for strength and power. But here he is, our Savior Jesus Christ. It is enough to make you weep.

Communion Prayer

Gentle Jesus, we come this day to the table of communion with eyes wide open to the miracle of redemption. We cry out for the suffering endured for the sins of the world. We long to turn instead to happier times and see your smiling face cradled in Mary's arms or your triumphant gaze beaming from the throne of God. But here at this place we see the depth of your devotion. Here is a love mingled with sweat. Here is a power strengthened by pain. Here is the Son of God present to us in the form of human flesh, body and blood.

We come to your table to eat of this bread and drink of this cup in remembrance of the presence of the living God. As we share in this meal we mourn for the sorrow of the world. We long for the presence of your touch to comfort our mourning and to guide us in the paths of righteousness. For to such belongs the realm of God. In our Savior's name we pray. Amen.

Suggestions for Celebration

Preparation: Put a picture or sculpture of the crucified Christ on the communion table. Read Isaiah 53:4–5. Sing "When I Survey the Wondrous Cross" (*Chalice Hymnal,* #195).

Celebration: Read the communion meditation and prayer. During communion, sing "When Jesus Wept" (*Chalice Hymnal,* #199).

Sharing Our Sorrows by Crying for the World

"Daughter, you are blessed when you weep, because grieving for people's sins will lead to saving many souls. So do not fear, daughter, for this is a singular and special gift from God."

Margery Kempe (p. 145)

With encouragement from her friends, Margery accepted her tears as a form of prayer. Julian of Norwich reminded her that when we do not know how to pray, the Spirit intercedes on our behalf with sighs too deep for words. Margery kept vigil at the bedside of the sick because her crying comforted the grieving. Once she was asked to cry at the scene of a church fire because the townsfolk believed her tears had the power to unleash showers from heaven. More often her ministry took traditional forms. She prayed at the side of a young mother plagued with depression, and she cared for her husband in his declining health. In her tears, she witnessed to the ability to share in the love of God.

Margery shows us that compassion can take many forms when we open ourselves to the power of the Holy Spirit. She trusted that even her tears could be a gift from God. To cry with others is to bear witness to their pain and to sigh with them in their agony. Such an act of service acknowledges that we do not know what to do, but we do know whom to trust. Paul reminds the Romans that the Spirit intercedes for the saints according to the will of God. It is this hope that we share.

Communion Meditation

As you approach this communion hour, take a moment to sigh for the sorrows of the world. Think of someone who is suffering in pain or is struggling with turmoil. You do not need to know how to solve the dilemma; you just need to feel the agony. The Spirit of God will see your tears. Your sighs will rise up from this communion table to settle in the bosom of our Creator. As a hen gathers her flock, so God will gather our prayers and shield them in Her mighty wings. There they will be gathered with the powers of the universe to set loose the will of God.

Let us gather at this table with the saints of all ages and take comfort in the knowledge of their triumphs. Taste in this bread the strength that supports their faith. Drink in this cup the power of the will of God. Feel in their witness the Body of Christ stretched throughout the ages to take away the sins of the world. Come to share in the feast of salvation.

Communion Prayer

Spirit of the living God, fall afresh on us. We come to you with sighs too deep for words, not knowing how to pray for the salvation that satisfies our world. Take from us our anguish on behalf of those we love. Fill their hearts with comfort and our souls with the assurance of your abiding care. Make this meal a reminder of the majesty of your power over death and the depth of your compassion for the lost. Nothing is outside your realm, and in this hope we place our trust. Make our tears into waters of redemption and our anguish into acts of compassion. For it is in the name of the One who shares with us in suffering love that we pray. Amen.

Suggestions for Celebration

Preparation: Read Romans 8:26–27. Take a few moments for silent prayer. Let the names of loved ones be spoken aloud. Read the quote about Margery Kempe as a prayer of assurance. Sing together "In Suff'ring Love" (*Chalice Hymnal*, #212).

Celebration: Read the communion meditation and prayer. Pass the elements of communion and wait to partake of them together. As you eat the bread say, "This is the bread of heaven." As you drink the cup say, "This is the cup of blessing."

Sharing Our Sorrows by Crying for Justice

*"Angels gather in chorus singing highest praise, yet the clouds cry
out in pain over the Innocents' blood."*

Hildegard of Bingen (Song lyrics in *Book of Divine Works*, p. 388)

Hildegard's vision of community always challenges the
imagination. Here she suggests that clouds lament the sorrows of
the world while angels herald the future victory of God with shouts
of glory. This harmony of lamentation and praise weaves the struggles
of the past into the hope of the future and places the community of
faith in the company of the heavens. With the expansion of the
dimensions of time and space, the blood of the innocents is
remembered and redeemed. The King of glory welcomes the faithful
while the tyrant of oppression is suffocated in death. And still
Hildegard concludes her song with the mournful refrain, "And the
clouds cry out in pain over the Innocents' blood."

With the clouds as witness to our sorrows, we gain a new
understanding of the forces of the universe. When we see rain thunder
forth from the sky, we can imagine the clouds crying out against
injustice. We know that rain is a natural phenomenon and is necessary
to the survival of our world. Yet it can also cause floods that ravage
the Earth. Now this natural cycle is put into a larger picture of the
cycle of justice and injustice. All the cycles of birth and death that
fill the Earth find their purpose in the will of God. To open our eyes
to this vision will not make everything right. But it may empower
us to remember the innocent of our time and sing with the angels.

Communion Meditation

The gospels are filled with references to the cosmos' awaiting
the realm of God. An angel announces to Mary the coming of the
Son of God. At his baptism the heavens part and confirm him with
a blessing. The sea is calmed by his touch. Fig trees are withered by
his curse. During his suffering the sky turns black, and at the moment
of his death the earth shakes. He ascends into the clouds and will
return with the clouds to create a new heaven and a new earth.

We stand at this table with all the cosmos. Heaven and earth meet in the breaking of this bread. The wheat of the fields and the fruit of the vineyard bear witness to the living presence of God. Wind and fire, water and earth wait patiently for the coming of the Lord. We are summoned by a bounteous harvest to bow down before the power of the universe and join in the mystery of salvation. Past and future, sorrow and joy, heaven and earth flow mingled down. All is one in the Body of Christ.

Communion Prayer

Alpha and Omega, meet us in this communion hour. In these precious moments open our eyes to your majesty. Let us hear the cries of the heavens and the songs of the angels. Let us never forget the suffering of the innocent and the promise of their victory. Fuel our hope with a glimpse of the transformation of the earth and the calming of the seas. In the taking of these elements let us feel the winds of the Spirit and taste the victory of your realm. In the company of this meal let us join with all creation to bear witness to the coming of our Lord. Amen.

Suggestions for Celebration

Preparation: Prepare the communion table with tokens that represent the elements of earth, wind, water, and fire. Lay these on cotton to represent the clouds and sprinkle the table with feathers to represent angels' wings. In the middle of the table place the bread and cup for communion.

Celebration: Read the communion meditation. Then read and sing the responsive reading "All Things New" (*Chalice Hymnal,* #702). Read the communion prayer. After communion, sing "When All Is Ended" (*Chalice Hymnal,* #703).

Sharing Our Sorrows by Petitioning God

"Catherine became a go-between, coming and going from our Lord to her mother, petitioning him and persuading her."

Raymond Capua (*Life of Catherine of Siena*, p. 230)

The record of Catherine's life is filled with testimonies to the power of her prayers, and her most fervent prayers were on behalf of her mother. As her mother slipped toward death, Catherine prayed, "Lord, this is not what you promised me." She constantly wrestled with God on behalf of those who suffered, and believed that her petitions would reach the heart of God. And those who knew Catherine believed God listened to her prayers. Her mother did recover, and her biographer wrote, "Nature bowed to God's command issued through the mouth of Catherine."

Many of us have lost the ability to pray for others. In our scientific age we have little faith in the power to defy the laws of nature. We believe in God but are reluctant to call on God to intervene in the sorrows of our lives. Yet each day we learn more and more about the intricate connections of mind, body, and spirit. Miracles are not the power to defy nature, but the power to see God at work in nature. Could there be some truth in the possibility of nature's bowing to God's command through the petition of faithful Christians? As we wrestle with this question let us remember the witness of those who benefited from the prayers of Catherine.

Communion Meditation

As we bring the sorrows of the world to the communion table, we remember the words of Jesus. When we pray we can seek and find, ask and receive, knock and have doors opened. Communion is a time to seek the presence of the living God and find answers for the sorrows of our world. It is an opportunity to ask for God's healing touch and receive the power of forgiveness. It is a place to knock on the door of God's heart and be opened to the power of God.

Come to this table ready to commune with God. Imagine what your prayers could unleash. Do not be afraid to wrestle with God on behalf of others. Remember the witness of Christians who have

118

fervently prayed for those they love. Jesus showed us how to trust in the power of prayer. Over a thousand years later, Catherine of Siena was still following his example. Let us join in the company of the faithful and share in our sorrows by believing in the transforming redemption of God.

Communion Prayer

Holy Spirit, Heavenly Dove, we long to feel your presence in this communion hour. Descend upon our hearts and breathe upon us your healing power. We lift up to your care our loved ones who languish in pain and illness. Help them to overcome the suffering of these days, and guide those who care for them with strength and compassion. Fill us with the fullness of your grace. We lift up to your care the weak and wounded of our community. Ease the torment of their lives and give their guardians wisdom to seek justice for their iniquities. Fill us with the fullness of your grace. We lift up to your care the factions of our church. Forgive us for our failure to bear witness to the unity of your love, and empower us with fervor for your realm. Fill us with the fullness of your grace. We lift to your care the hatred of our world. Bring to light the prejudices that fuel discrimination, and set before us a path for reconciliation. Fill us with the fullness of your grace. We praise you for all that we receive, thank you for all we find, and look forward to all that is opened by your grace. In the name of the One who taught us how to commune with you we pray. Amen.

Suggestions for Celebration

Preparation: Read Luke 11:9–13. Read the communion meditation. Sing together "Spirit, Come, Dispel Our Sadness" (*Chalice Hymnal,* #253).

Celebration: Read the communion prayer. After communion, sing together the hymn "Sweet, Sweet Spirit" (*Chalice Hymnal,* #261).

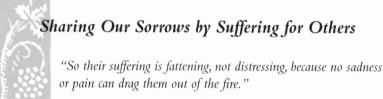

Sharing Our Sorrows by Suffering for Others

"So their suffering is fattening, not distressing, because no sadness or pain can drag them out of the fire."

Catherine of Siena (*Dialogue*, p. 147)

Sharing in the sorrows of the world was not only a Christian duty but a means to strengthening Catherine's faith. She called sadness "fattening" to suggest that it enlarges our outlook and our faith. To feel sorrow for another's pain, to anguish at the harm done to our neighbors, to grieve with the sick and dying is hard, and Catherine admits that it makes her sad. But she writes that this is not a sadness that dries up her soul; rather it strengthens it in love. Catherine takes comfort in the witness of Christ, who bore the sorrow of his suffering for others, both in his pain on the cross and his longing for the redemption of the world. It is through love for others that we are set afire with holy love. For Catherine, there is no other way to commune with God.

Every day we see examples of people with extraordinary faith who share in the sorrows of others. Daughters and sons give loving care to parents who linger on the borders between life and death. Those who watch from afar admire their devotion and murmur about the sacrifice they are making. And indeed the decision to care for an ailing relative is hard. It requires devotion and sacrifice, but it can also be deeply joyful and satisfying. Caregivers speak of the opportunity to see every moment of life as precious. They find inner strength they never knew they possessed. And in the face of the dying, they see a glimpse of the face of God. In the sadness of pain, they burn brightly in holy love.

Communion Meditation

No one wants to suffer. Certainly Jesus did not want to endure the suffering of the cross. But he did, and because of his willingness to enter fully into the depths of human life, we are given a new vision of life. This life that we celebrate is a life full of the love of God. It is a love centered in the hope of God's enduring presence. It is a hope that forms the center of our existence. It is an existence that can endure. This endurance can stand the pain of suffering. In this we find our peace.

At this table, we honor all those who are alive in the love of God. We are grateful for family members who care for the dying, for hospice workers and palliative care teams who bring comfort and dignity to life, for social workers who bring hope to troubled families, for counselors who listen to the distressed, for pastors and teachers who preach good news to the world in the midst of it all. In these people, we see the body of our risen Lord. Come drink of the love of God.

Communion Prayer

Loving God, we gather at this table full of the memory of eternal love. We thank you for the love of salvation that burns brightly through the agony of the cross, bearing witness to the flame of everlasting life. We see around us loving souls set afire with the passion of your justice. Give us the courage to listen to their cries on behalf of the weary. Strengthen our resolve to warm our own hearts in the love of our neighbor. Meet us in this communion hour, and burn within us as we dare to be shaped in the furnace of your love. In Jesus' name we pray. Amen.

Suggestions for Celebration

Preparation: Set a Christ candle in the middle of the communion table. Surround it with candles. Read Romans 5:1–5. Read the communion meditation and then light the Christ candle. Sing together "Holy and Good Is the Gift of Desire" (*Chalice Hymnal,* #509).

Celebration: Come to the communion table to partake in the elements of communion. Light a candle from the Christ candle and return to your seat for silent prayer. At the end of communion, sing the chorus of "I Am the Light of the World!" (*Chalice Hymnal,* #469).

Sharing Our Sorrows by Hoping for Victory

"He will be defeated, not by what our bodies suffer, but by virtue of the glowing measureless Charity of God. Amen. Sweet Jesus. Jesus, Love."

Catherine of Siena
(in writings edited by Foster, pp. 276-77)

These are the last words that Catherine wrote to her dear friend Raymond. The two of them had worked together to reform the church. They shared a passion to sweep the church clean of corruption. They had encountered much resistance and shared in the sorrow of the church's continued divisions. Catherine was so weak from the fight that she knew she would die. Yet her thoughts were not on the many defeats they had endured, but on the ultimate victory of the realm of God. Just as Christ defeated the devil in the resurrection, she observes, so he will defeat the demons of the present age. She urges Raymond to carry on after her death by staying true to their vision for reform and by receiving communion every day. Take courage in Christ Jesus, she writes, and have no regrets.

After her death, Raymond placed his hope in keeping Catherine's memory alive. He wrote a biography of her life to document her piety and to spread her message of reform. Her letters and prayers were copied and sent to her followers to encourage their faith. Catherine's status as a saint and doctor of theology is due to his efforts and the hope that the two of them shared in the measureless love of God. They speak across the ages to all who labor on behalf of the gospel and share in the hope of faith.

We who find our home in the community of faith share the sorrows of a church rent asunder by scandal and corruption. The church still is divided in spirit and in truth. We preach the love of God, yet we cannot even share in communion as one Body of Christ. The scandal of our division could defeat us, were it not for the hope of our future redemption. As we mourn over the pain of our present community, let us keep alive the hope of our foundation in the oneness of the living God.

Communion Meditation

In these words from the letter to the Romans, Paul expresses the hope of Christian faith. In light of this assurance that nothing can separate us from the love of God, we can see clearly the majesty and magnitude of our salvation. No earthly suffering is below it; no heavenly body is above it. There is no time outside it, nor any earthly power beyond it. The heights and the depths of the universe rest in God. And for this victory, sealed for us in the life, death, and resurrection of Jesus Christ, we lift our hearts in praise.

Communion Prayers

Before Communion: Rock of Salvation, we gather this day at your table of blessing. We come from the storms that rage in our world and the winds that beat our community to seek solace in your abiding care. In this bread and this cup, we taste the righteousness of the living God. We praise you for the nourishment of this community of faith, which comforts us in sorrow and shares our pain. We pray that our hearts will be strengthened by this manifestation of your grace. In the glory of your name we pray. Amen.

After Communion: Sweet Jesus, truly nothing is as sweet as the communion of the Body of Christ. Forgive us for the divisions that keep your church from gathering as one body around this table. Help us keep our eyes focused on your face and our feet planted in your holy Word. With our strength renewed, lead us forward to the ultimate victory of your realm. For thine is the kingdom and the power and the glory, forever and ever. Amen.

Suggestions for Celebration

Preparation: Read Romans 8:38–39. Read the communion meditation. Sing verses one through three of "My Hope Is Built" (*Chalice Hymnal,* #537).

Celebration: Read the prayer before communion. After sharing in communion, read the concluding prayer. Sing verse four of the hymn.

Sharing Our Sorrows by Shining in Splendor

"But then three great stars, crowding together in their brilliance, appear in the darkness, and then many others, both small and large, shining with great splendor."

Hildegard of Bingen (*Scivias*, p. 153)

Our meditations end where they began, with Hildegard's vision of light. Here she sees salvation emerge as lights that shine in the darkness of sin. The first lights are preludes to the coming of the Messiah. These three represent Abraham, Isaac, and Jacob, but they symbolize the work of the Trinity in all people who walk in the light. Their works of faith light up the sky. Their faces shine with the goodness of their faith. With each new generation the light of salvation burns brighter until, gathered in the Word of God, the darkness is overcome.

During the season of Advent the church celebrates the coming of the realm of God. It gathers in the dark of winter to celebrate the light of present salvation and future hope. Each time we celebrate communion we search for this light that is with us and yet beyond our reach. As we feel the presence of the Body of Christ, our lives shine forth with his light. As we share in the sorrows of the world, we look to Jesus as the lamp that lights our way. He is the light of the world. And we who follow it will share in the light of life.

Communion Meditation

On the communion table this day we see an Advent wreath with candles for hope, peace, love, and joy gathered around the Christ candle. As we light each candle, think of someone who represents for you the work of faith. As you look at the candle of hope, remember the strength that you have gained from someone who brought hope to your life. As you think of those who have shared the peace of Christ with you, utter thanks for their works of mercy. In the candle of love see blazing the hearts of those who care for you each day. In joy give thanks for this community with which you share the light of life.

124

Each person in this room bears witness to the light of the world. We who receive the light of Christ shine in his light. We are beacons of hope for the hopeless, bearers of peace to the war torn, vessels of love for the brokenhearted, and witnesses of joy in the world. Let us burn forever bright in the light of salvation and one by one fill the sky with the radiance of the reign of God.

Communion Prayer

Light of the world, shine forth on this community of faith. We see gathered at this table the lives of the faithful as stars in the heaven full of the light of your grace. In the face of each smiling child we see the radiance of your face. In the lives of the faithful through the ages we witness the brightness of your salvation. In the witness of the Son of God we see the lamp that guides our feet and the light that illumines our path. Shine in us; shine in the heavens; shine through the darkness; shine to the ends of creation. Shine forth and light the world. Amen.

Suggestions for Celebration

Preparation: Put an Advent wreath on the communion table. Light the Christ candle. Then read the communion meditation, lighting each candle as you meditate on its meaning. Take time to read the meditation slowly, pausing between each phrase. Sing together "One Candle Is Lit" (*Chalice Hymnal,* #128).

Celebration: Read the communion prayer. After communion, read John 8:12.

BIBLIOGRAPHY

Bell, John. *Psalms of David and Songs of Mary.* The Cathedral Singers. GIA Publications, 1997.

Bondi, Roberta. *Memories of God: Theological Reflections on a Life.* Nashville: Abingdon Press, 1995.

Catherine of Siena. *The Dialogue.* Translated by Suzanne Noffke. New York: Paulist Press, 1980.

————. *I, Catherine: Selected Writings of St. Catherine of Siena.* Edited and translated by Kenelm Foster and Mary John Ronayne. London: Collins Co., 1980.

————. *The Letters of St. Catherine of Siena.* Vol. 1. Translated by Suzanne Noffke. Binghamton, New York: Medieval and Renaissance Texts and Studies, 1988.

Chalice Hymnal. St. Louis: Chalice Press, 1995.

Chalice Worship. Edited by Colbert Cartwright and O. I. Cricket Harrison. St. Louis: Chalice Press, 1997.

Hadewijch of Brabant. *The Complete Works.* Translated by Mother Columba Hart. New York: Paulist Press, 1980.

Harrison, Beverly. "The Power of Anger in the Work of Love." In *Weaving the Visions: New Patterns in Feminist Spirituality.* Edited by Carol Christ and Judith Plaskow, pp. 214–55. San Francisco: Harper and Row, 1989.

Heyward, Carter. *Saving Jesus From Those Who Are Right: Rethinking What It Means to be Christian.* Minneapolis: Fortress Press, 1999.

Hildegard of Bingen. *Book of Divine Works with Letters and Songs.* Edited by Matthew Fox. Santa Fe, N. Mex.: Bear and Company, 1987.

————. *The Book of the Rewards of Life.* Translated by Bruce Hozeski. New York: Oxford University Press, 1994.

————. *Scivias.* Translated by Mother Columba Hart and Jane Bishop. New York: Paulist Press, 1990.

Johnson, Elizabeth. *Friends of God and Prophets: A Feminist Theological Reading of the Communion of Saints.* New York: Continuum, 1998.

Julian of Norwich. *Showings.* Translated by Edmund Colledge and James Walsh. New York: Paulist Press, 1978.

Kempe, Margery. *The Book of Margery Kempe*. Translated by John Skinner. New York: Image Books, 1998.

Larson, Lloyd. *The Lord Is My Shepherd*. Delaware Water Gap, Penn.: GlorySound, 1993.

McAvoy, Jane. *The Satisfied Life: Medieval Women Mystics on Atonement*. Cleveland: The Pilgrim Press, 2000.

Mechthild of Magdeburg. *The Flowing Light of the Godhead*. Translated by Frank Tobin. New York: Paulist Press, 1998.

Pelikan, Jaroslav. *Mary Through the Centuries: Her Place in the History of Culture*. New Haven, Conn.: Yale University Press, 1996.

Petroff, Elizabeth Alvilda. *Medieval Women's Visionary Literature*. New York: Oxford University Press, 1986.

Raymond of Capua. *The Life of Catherine of Siena*. Translated by Conleth Kearns. Wilmington, Del.: Michael Glazier, 1980.

Schwartz, Stephen. *Godspell: A Musical Based Upon the Gospel According to St. Matthew*. Cast recording. Arista, 1990.

Simon, Paul, and Art Garfunkel. *Bridge Over Troubled Water*. Sony/Columbia Records, 1987.

Souther, Richard. *Vision: The Music of Hildegard von Bingen*. Angel Records, 1995.

INDEX OF HYMNS AND READINGS

A   *Page*

A Mighty Fortress Is Our God (*Chalice Hymnal,* #65)   25
All Earth Is Waiting (*Chalice Hymnal,* #139)   47
All Things New (*Chalice Hymnal,* #702)   117
All the Way My Savior Leads Me (*Chalice Hymnal,* #559)   55
All Who Hunger, Gather Gladly (*Chalice Hymnal,* #419)   43
An Upper Room Did Our Lord Prepare (*Chalice Hymnal,* #385)   29

B

Blest Be the Tie That Binds (*Chalice Hymnal,* #433)   81
Bread of the World, in Mercy Broken (*Chalice Hymnal,* #387)   49

C

Come, Share the Lord (*Chalice Hymnal,* #408)   91

D

Draw Us in the Spirit's Tether (*Chalice Hymnal,* #392)   83

F

Fill My Cup, Lord (*Chalice Hymnal,* #351)   103

G

Give Thanks (*Chalice Hymnal,* #528)   77

H

Help Us Accept Each Other (*Chalice Hymnal,* #487)   41
Her Baby, Newly Breathing (*Chalice Hymnal,* #158)   75
Holy and Good Is the Gift of Desire (*Chalice Hymnal,* #509)   121

I

I Am the Light of the World! (*Chalice Hymnal,* #469)   121
I Am Thine, O Lord (*Chalice Hymnal,* #601)   101
I Bind My Heart This Tide (*Chalice Hymnal,* #350)   99
I Come with Joy (*Chalice Hymnal,* #420)   39
I Would Be True (*Chalice Hymnal,* #608)   97
In Christ There Is No East or West (*Chalice Hymnal,* #687)   49
In Suff'ring Love (*Chalice Hymnal,* #212)   115

Page

Infant Holy, Infant Lowly (*Chalice Hymnal,* #163)   65
It Is Well with My Soul (*Chalice Hymnal,* #561)   33

J

Jesus, Lover of My Soul (*Chalice Hymnal,* #542)   67
Joy to the World (*Chalice Hymnal,* #143)   69

L

Lead On, O King Eternal (*Chalice Hymnal,* #632)   99
Let All Mortal Flesh Keep Silence (*Chalice Hymnal,* #124)   75
Let Us Talents and Tongues Employ (*Chalice Hymnal,* #422)   53
like a child (*Chalice Hymnal,* #133)   65
Lo, How a Rose E'er Blooming (*Chalice Hymnal,* #160)   85
Lo, I Am with You (*Chalice Hymnal,* #430)   59

M

May the Blessing of God (*Chalice Hymnal,* #448)   103
Mothering God, You Gave Me Birth (*Chalice Hymnal,* #83)   61
My Hope Is Built (*Chalice Hymnal,* #537)   123
My Soul Gives Glory to My God (*Chalice Hymnal,* #130)   77

N

Now the Green Blade Rises (*Chalice Hymnal,* #230)   89

O

O Christ, the Way, the Truth, the Life (*Chalice Hymnal,* #432)   55
O God of Vision (*Chalice Hymnal,* #288)   81
O Love That Wilt Not Let Me Go (*Chalice Hymnal,* #540)   21
O Morning Star (*Chalice Hymnal,* #105)   69
On Eagle's Wings (*Chalice Hymnal,* #77)   23
One Bread, One Body (*Chalice Hymnal,* #393)   17
Open My Eyes, That I May See (*Chalice Hymnal,* #586)   95

P

Prayer for Healing (*Chalice Hymnal,* #505)   63

R

Restless Weaver (*Chalice Hymnal,* #658)   79

Page

S

Seed, Scattered and Sown (*Chalice Hymnal*, #395)	109
Sheaves of Summer (*Chalice Hymnal*, #396)	57
Silence, Frenzied, Unclean Spirit! (*Chalice Hymnal*, #186)	41
Sing of a God in Majestic Divinity (*Chalice Hymnal*, #331)	95
Sing of Mary, Pure and Lowly (*Chalice Hymnal*, #184)	73
Sister, Let Me Be Your Servant (*Chalice Hymnal*, #490)	111
Softly and Tenderly (*Chalice Hymnal*, #340)	35
Song of Mary (*Chalice Hymnal*, #131)	77
Spirit, Come, Dispel Our Sadness (*Chalice Hymnal*, #253)	119
Spirit of the Living God (*Chalice Hymnal*, #259)	57
Strong, Gentle Children (*Chalice Hymnal*, #511)	37
Sweet, Sweet Spirit (*Chalice Hymnal*, #261)	119

T

The Beatitudes (*Chalice Hymnal*, #185)	97
The Blood Will Never Lose Its Power (*Chalice Hymnal*, #206)	63
The Lord's Prayer (*Chalice Hymnal*, #310)	15
There Is a Balm in Gilead (*Chalice Hymnal*, #501)	63
There's a Wideness in God's Mercy (*Chalice Hymnal*, #73)	19
These I Lay Down (*Chalice Hymnal*, #391)	13
They'll Know We Are Christians (*Chalice Hymnal*, #494)	107

W

We Are Not Our Own (*Chalice Hymnal*, #689)	45
We Shall Overcome (*Chalice Hymnal*, #630)	29
Weave (*Chalice Hymnal*, #495)	107
Were You There (*Chalice Hymnal*, #198)	73
What a Friend We Have in Jesus (*Chalice Hymnal*, #585)	59
What Wondrous Love is This (*Chalice Hymnal*, #200)	23
When All Is Ended (*Chalice Hymnal*, #703)	117
When I Survey the Wondrous Cross (*Chalice Hymnal*, #195)	113
When Jesus Wept (*Chalice Hymnal*, #199)	113
Who Is My Mother, Who Is My Brother? (*Chalice Hymnal*, #486)	93
Womb of Life, and Source of Being (*Chalice Hymnal*, #14)	85

Y

You Satisfy the Hungry Heart (*Chalice Hymnal*, #429)	43

INDEX OF SCRIPTURE REFERENCES

Genesis 32:24–31	101	John 1:1–5	53
Psalm 23	15	John 1:4–5	69
Song of Solomon	67	John 6:48–51	103
Isaiah 53:4–5	113	John 8:12	125
Matthew 5	97	John 14:6	54
Matthew 11:28–30	35	John 15:12–17	67
Matthew 13:3–9, 18–23	89	John 17	27
Matthew 18:20	83	Acts 2:43–47	79
Matthew 25:31–46	79	Romans 5:1–5	121
Matthew 26:36–39	101	Romans 8:18–25	47
Matthew 28:20	59	Romans 8:26	52
Mark 1:21–28	41	Romans 8:26–27	115
Mark 3:31–35	93	Romans 8:38–39	123
Mark 9:33–37	99	Romans 9:3, 15	107
Mark 12:30	95	1 Corinthians 6:15, 20	43
Mark 14:22–25	9	1 Corinthians 10:16–17	109
Mark 15:33–41	73	1 Corinthians 11:17–32	27
Luke 1:26–38	75	1 Corinthians 11:23–26	9
Luke 1:42	85	1 Corinthians 11:27–33	45
Luke 1:46–55	76	1 Corinthians 12	17
Luke 2:14–19	73	1 Corinthians 13:9–12	81
Luke 2:25–38	65	2 Corinthians 5:16–20	49
Luke 6:37–38	91	Galatians 3:28	29
Luke 11:9–13	119	Hebrews 12:1–2	2
Luke 13:18–21	57	James 5:13–16	111
Luke 15:8–10	69	1 Peter 2:24	63
Luke 15:8–32	33